You Mean The Bible Teaches That...

You Mean The Bible Teaches That...

Charles Caldwell Ryrie

moody press
chicago

To

Elizabeth, Bruce, and Carolyn

*May you always ask the right questions
and heed His answers.*

Contents

Preface

THIS BOOK about questions people ask is motivated by the desire to investigate and try to communicate what God's Word says on these topics. The choice of the particular questions to be included was mine, based on those which often come up in meetings and aided by the suggestions of the publisher. There easily came to mind other questions that might have been included, as well as aspects of these that are discussed that could have been pursued further. However, the purpose has been to try to focus on the major aspects of problems which confront people today. Some of the chapters are basically theological, some are exegetical, while others are ethical and relate both to general and special ethics, including both social and personal. Hopefully the reader will be able to tolerate any disunity that this variety causes.

Chapters one, two, and ten have been published before (in *Bibliotheca Sacra*), but they have been revised (and used by permission) for this book. The others are new. There is not agreement about the many interpretations involved in these questions, but I have tried to give alternative views along with my own preferences, even though there are many places where one cannot be dogmatic. However, whether or not the reader agrees, it is imperative for all of us to try to know what God is saying about these matters in relation to our own time. The Bible does not deal with all possible situations that can arise in the ethical areas. Nevertheless, the wise Christian will seek to be Christlike, to try to think God's thoughts after Him and to lovingly apply the truth to each situation. Hopefully this book will help in understanding what the biblical teaching is, so that speaking the truth in love we may grow up in every way unto Him who is our Head.

1

The Question of Civil Obedience

THE ISSUE OF CIVIL DISOBEDIENCE versus civil obedience has affected many areas of life in this century. The riots of the sixties produced headlines like these: *Newly-formed "High School Rights Coalition" Announces Plans for Free-Speech Drive;* and *Bible College Students Participate in Demonstration.* After the '68 riot, Chicago Seven defense attorney Kunstler said, "If violence is the only way to get social order then I'll support it." This statement did not come from an ideological communistic revolutionary in some foreign country, but from a United States citizen who practices law. Politicians, judges, sociologists, and educators have all been drawn into the debate. Many psychologists seem to be dedicated to the proposition that everybody ought to be able to do his own thing in his own way and that no one should be blamed for his action.

It is not always easy to think clearly about the matter of civil disobedience when, for instance, our Lord Himself is sometimes pictured as a revolutionary who conspired in His day to overthrow the government. Since what happened in the sixties is not so widespread today, it affords a good opportunity to take a dispassionate look at the subject. Is a

Portions of this chapter, with minor changes, are reprinted from Charles C. Ryrie, "The Christian and Civil Disobedience," *Bibliotheca Sacra* 127 (April-June 1970): 153-62. Used by permission.

believer ever justified in breaking the law, especially in promoting causes which seem to demonstrate the chief characteristic of Christianity, namely, love? If, for example, it is right and even desirable for Christians in the South to demonstrate and lobby against liquor and gambling, then shouldn't Christians in the North do the same against racial and social injustices?

It is not easy to think clearly about these matters, but think we must. Those who campaign for civil disobedience have marshaled their arguments, and we need to know what's right or wrong about them.

The Influence of Henry David Thoreau

One champion of civil disobedience who is quite popular with young people on our campuses is the nineteenth-century New England writer, Henry David Thoreau. A humanist (in that man, not God, was his primary concern) and an idealist, Thoreau had a profound influence on many. For instance, Gandhi printed and distributed Thoreau's essay "Civil Disobedience" in pamphlet form and always carried a copy with him during his many imprisonments. Walt Whitman put his finger on Thoreau's continuing and current appeal when he said, "One thing about Thoreau keeps him very near to me: I refer to his lawlessness—his dissent—his going his absolute own road." And one of his biographers wrote: "Rare is the issue of an anarchist magazine in this country or abroad that does not somewhere in it cite him."

What did this man do and say that encourages the cause of civil disobedience in our day? His famous essay "On the Duty of Civil Disobedience" was occasioned by a night in the Concord jail. It all came about in July 1846 when

Thoreau refused to pay his poll tax as a protest against a government that supported slavery. Three years before, a close friend had done the same thing, and his example undoubtedly gave Thoreau needed courage! At any rate, the town constable offered to pay the tax, but Thoreau refused to let him. Nevertheless, during the night someone (probably his aunt) paid it for him, thus thwarting his efforts to protest his government's actions. The essay grew out of this experience and attempted to set his case before the people. Actually it does not focus on specific political issues but aims to wean men away from their adherence to an insidious relativism (government) and to persuade them to return to the superior standard of absolute truth (humanism). Though many argued even in his day that when moral law and government are in conflict, men should obey the government, Thoreau insisted that "it is not desirable to cultivate a respect for the law, so much as for the right." Furthermore, the most effective method of defending the right, in his judgment, was by civil disobedience—refusing to pay taxes, going to jail, even martyrdom.

All of this sounds very noble—and contemporary—but there's a very basic flaw in its approach. Who decides what is right? Government may very well be wrong, but is the individual's "own innate sense of goodness" (to which Thoreau appealed) necessarily any better? And which individual's sense of right should we follow? John Brown and John Jones may take exactly opposite points of view on the same issue, each feeling in his heart that he is right. Whom do we follow? And if we don't agree with either of them, then what? If three people practice civil disobedience, that's not so bad, but if three million try to do what is right in their own eyes, then civil disobedience becomes civil anarchy, because there may be three million different approaches! Thoreau's idealism may sound good, but when coupled with his humanism, it provides a standard no better than the human being who tries to practice it.

Two years before the poll tax and jail incident, Thoreau had another experience which is sometimes used as an example of a good thing to do when one is dissatisfied with the government. He moved into some woods on the shore of Walden Pond about a mile and a half from Concord, built a cabin, cultivated a garden, and in general simplified his life for two years, two months, and a few days. The experiences of those days he wrote of in *Walden*. He himself said, however, that he did not intend to suggest this kind of life for any who were satisfied with their present existence, nor did he advocate leaving home and family or abandoning civilization. During those years he did not isolate himself from his friends, whom he regularly visited in the evenings (since he was only a short distance from town), and while he despaired often of the so-called improvements of civilization, he advocated improving our spiritual natures as well as our material world. So his experiences at Walden Pond were not really an example of withdrawing from society, nor did they bear any resemblance to a present-day communal settlement.

But what Thoreau did illustrate is exactly what is often practiced today—humanistic ethics, or let everybody do his own thing in his own way without blame. That is the question at the heart of civil disobedience: Does an individual have the right to put his will above the government under which he lives and follow whatever course of action he thinks proper? Humanism is the philosophic basis for most civil disobedience, albeit humanism in varying degrees of altruism or selfishness. The arguments go like this. If a law is clearly unconstitutional, then it must be broken in order to test it or protest it. But who decides if a law is clearly unconstitutional? Is this up to each individual, or do we abide by the decisions of the courts? And if someone does decide that he must break a law in order to test it, he of course must be prepared to pay the penalty. Furthermore, it is very important to remember these days that testing a law under our legal system does not require *mass* violations of it in order to bring it to a test.

Or sometimes we hear advocates of civil disobedience justifying their actions on the basis of using that means only as a last resort. But again, who determines when all legal means have been exhausted? This is a subjective humanistic judgment.

Or again we are told that acts of civil disobedience are permissible as long as the participant is willing to take the punishment. This seems to be a perfectly justifiable stance except for the fact that punishment has commonly been regarded in all societies as just retribution for a crime and not a perfectly respectable choice of action open to anyone. In other words, the fact that someone is willing to take the punishment does not make his crime respectable.

That word *crime* brings up a point that is often overlooked by civil disobedience movements. Acts of civil disobedience are crimes. Protests may not be crimes, depending on the laws of the land and the conduct of the protestors, but violations of the law are illegal actions, however they may be justified in the minds of the violators.

The Biblical Teaching

For a Christian there should be no question about the

basis for guiding his relationship to the government under which he lives. He does not—indeed, cannot—operate on a subjective basis, nor can he espouse a humanistic ethic. It is the Bible which guides all of his conduct, and the Bible has a good deal to say by way of direct teaching and example about the matter of civil disobedience.

The teaching of Christ. The Lord recognized the dual citizenship of His followers in His classic statement: "Render to Caesar the things that are Caesar's, and to God the things that are God's" (Mk 12:17). He also made it clear that God's servants do not fight in order to bring in the spiritual kingdom (Jn 18:36), although soldiers, even repentant ones, are a legitimate part of the order of this world's kingdoms (Lk 3:14). Failure to make this distinction has led some to picture our Lord as a revolutionary and a leader in civil disobedience. He is described by some as a serious threat to established law and order or as conspiring to overthrow the established government. To be sure, our Lord was a threat to the religious establishment of His day, but not to the political kingdom of Rome, and Pilate clearly recognized that (Jn 18:33-38). Jesus was not an anarchist trying to overthrow Rome, nor did He spend His time protesting the political sins of Rome.

The teaching of the apostles. The apostles give the Christian clear guidelines about obeying government. Paul commanded believers to be submissive to the government (Ro 13:1-7) because authority is ordained of God (v. 1, and notice that nothing is said about only certain forms of government being ordained of God); because resistance to government is in the final analysis resistance to God (v. 2); because government generally opposes evil (v. 4); and because our consciences tell us to obey (v. 5). No exceptions are listed to these reasons for obeying that would justify civil disobedience.

Eight or nine years later, after having much personal involvement (including several imprisonments) with the Roman government under which he lived, Paul had not changed his mind about the teaching he had written before in Romans. He said again essentially the same things: "Put them in mind to be subject [this is the same verb as in Romans 13:1] to principalities and powers [this is also the same word as in the previous passage], to obey magistrates, to be ready to every good work" (Titus 3:1). Maltreatment at the hands of the Roman government had evidently not provided Paul with sufficient existential grounds for changing his teaching (see also 1 Th 2:2).

About the same time as Paul was writing to Titus, Peter wrote a similar word on submitting to government (1 Pe 2:13-17). The reasons he listed for obeying are that by obeying God-ordained government we show our obedience to God Himself (v. 13); that it is the will of God (v. 15); and that it is a part of a good testimony to the unsaved (v. 15). This obedience, according to Peter, should extend to every ordinance and to all rulers. Again no exceptions are indicated either because of the type of government or because of the conscience of the believer. Actually the principle underlying this concept of civil obedience is the believer's position as a servant of God (v. 16). In summary, the direct teaching of Scripture seems to require complete civil obedience on the part of Christians.

Both the Pauline and Petrine teaching were written under the reign of the emperor Nero (54-68). Romans was written during the first period of his reign, the celebrated quinquennium, which was characterized by good government and popularity. It is reported that Seneca said of Nero that he was incapable of learning cruelty. Royal intrigue, however, led by his mother, resulted in her death in A.D. 60 and in a definite change of pattern of life and government on the part of Nero. He plunged deeper and deeper into personal dissipation and brought the empire bankruptcy. On July 18, A.D. 64, Rome began to burn. Whatever Nero's part may or may not have been in this, the populace wanted a scapegoat, and suspicion surrounded Nero. To divert this from himself, he attempted to lay the blame on the Christians. Tacitus described the process this way:

> Wherefore in order to allay the rumor he [Nero] put forward as guilty, and afflicted with the most exquisite punishments those who were hated for their abominations and called "Christians" by the populace. . . . Therefore first of all those who confessed [to being Christians] were arrested, and then as a result of their information a large number were implicated, not so much on the charge of incendiarism as for hatred of the human race. They died by methods of mockery; some were covered with the skins of wild beasts and then torn by dogs, some were crucified, some were burned as torches to give light at night. . . . men felt that their destruction was not on account of the public welfare but to gratify the cruelty of one [Nero].[1]

Many place the writing of 1 Peter shortly after the beginning of this Neronian persecution. If Peter was in Rome at this time (which seems likely from 1 Pe 5:13), this makes his teaching about civil obedience even more significant.

Examples of disobedience. But, you ask, are there not examples of civil disobedience in the Bible? Didn't Peter say that we ought to obey God rather than man (Ac 5:29)?

Yes he did, and in regard to the authority of the Sanhedrin, which had not only religious power but also wide political power at the time of Christ's life. This, therefore, is a legitimate example of the principle that disobedience of authority is justified when that authority requires a believer to disobey the laws of God.

Shadrach, Meshach, and Abednego disobeyed the king when they were brought into direct conflict with Nebuchadnezzar's decree to worship the golden image (Dan 3). Daniel, too, disobeyed when the law of the land brought him into direct conflict with the revealed law of God (Dan 6). In both instances God vindicated their stand by delivering them miraculously from the punishment. This, however, was not always the case. "Others were tortured . . . others had trial of cruel mockings and scourgings . . . of bonds and imprisonment: they were stoned, they were sawn asunder, were tempted, were slain with the sword . . . being destitute, afflicted, tormented" (Heb 11:35-37). Even legitimate disobedience does not automatically bring exemption from punishment.

At Philippi, Paul insisted that the Roman authorities should do their God-appointed job properly and not rule unrighteously (Ac 16:37). Indeed, one might say that Paul was responsible for a sit-in, for he refused to move until the authorities came and apologized. He was trying to compel the authorities to fulfill their God-appointed task; he did not sit in because of a selfish claim against the authorities.

When civil law and God's law are in opposition, the illustrations of the Bible sanction, if not obligate, the believer to protest or disobey. But when a believer feels he should disobey his government, he must be sure it is not because the government has denied him *his* rights, but because it has denied him *God's* rights.[2]

THE CONTEMPORARY RAMIFICATION OF THE DOCTRINE OF OBEDIENCE

The doctrine of civil obedience is but a part of the larger teaching of Scripture on subjection to constituted authority. Angelic beings are subject to Christ (1 Pe 3:22); believers are to be subject to one another (1 Pe 5:5); the church is subject to Christ (Eph 5:24); the Son shall be subject to the Father (1 Co 15:28); servants are subject to their masters (1 Pe 2:18); children are under their parents (1 Ti 3:4); wives are subject to their husbands (Col 3:18); young people are to be subject to their elders (1 Pe 5:5); church members are to be governed by their leaders (Heb 13:7, 17); and believers are to be subject to their government. It is part of a total doctrine of obedience.

One cannot deny the fact that the various areas in which authority is established are interrelated in the Scriptures. Therefore, a breakdown in one area will involve breakdowns in others, and this is exactly what is happening in our contemporary society. Civil disobedience, ecclesiastical disobedience, disobedience in the home are interrelated. Since this is true, the Christian should demonstrate orderliness within the various spheres to which he is related. When he is under authority he should submit obediently; when he is in authority, he should lead with justice. It is nothing short of hypocrisy for a Christian to decry public acts of disobedience while he perpetrates private ones.

THE ESCHATOLOGICAL RAMIFICATION OF DISOBEDIENCE

The world seems to be plunging rapidly down the path

of increasing lawlessness in many areas of life. Where will it all end? The Bible answers that question quite plainly and vividly in 2 Timothy 3:1-5. There are listed eighteen characteristics of the hard times of the last days, and many of them reflect lawlessness. Blasphemy is lawlessness against God; disobedience to parents is lawlessness in the family; without natural affection is lawlessness against one's own body; trucebreaking is lawlessness with others; fierce means untamed, which speaks for itself; despisers of those that are good refers to lawlessness in respect to the established order; heady means reckless, and so it goes. No city, no country, no class, no institution will be exempt from this rampant lawlessness.

I can think of no situation into which a dictator could more easily move than this state of lawlessness. Perhaps you read the book or saw the telecast of *The Rise and Fall of the Third Reich*. The pieces of that picture should never have fit together. There was the unknown fanatic who was disliked and distrusted by almost everyone except his small band of followers; there were intelligent, civilized, and cultured people who should have seen what was happening; and there was a democratic government that should have prevented such a takeover. The pieces would not have fit together except for one ingredient which was present in the situation, and that was lawlessness. In the wake of lawlessness, Hitler was swept to power. The impossible happened, and the lawless situation was replaced by the law of a lawless dictator. And this is exactly what will happen on a worldwide scale before long. The lawlessness of our day is ripening the world for a takeover by some who will promise to bring order, even by the use of force, out of this chaos. Such a one will arise—to be sure, after the church has gone to meet the Lord in the air—and, paradoxically, he is called the lawless one (2 Th 2:8). History will repeat itself, only this time on a much larger scale. Christians today must be certain that they are not contributing to this climate of lawlessness in any sphere of life.

Is not the Christian to take leadership in trying to correct the ills of society, and will not this responsibility sometimes involve and justify acts of civil disobedience? Certainly the believer has a social responsibility, and in a word it is to do good to all men and especially to other believers. But he also has a civic responsibility, and that is to be an obedient citizen. If the government under which he lives allows for means of legitimate protest and change, he surely may use them. But to take the law into his own hands finds no support in the Scriptures. The only exception seems to be if the government forbids his worshiping God. To serve Caesar and even fight for him, the Christian must do; to worship Caesar, he must not do. It is instructive to remember that the New Testament writers did not crusade against one of the worst social ills of their day—slavery. Paul advised Christian slaves not to let it matter to them (1 Co 7:22). He did not advise them to become martyrs in the cause of liberation. Indeed, even when writing to a Christian master about a runaway slave who had become a believer, he only suggests that he be taken back and not punished. He never even hints that the master should free his slaves because this was the Christian thing to do (Phile 17).

The Christian's primary responsibilities are evangelism and godly living. Through witnessing he changes men; through righteous living he affects society; through private and public obedience he honors God.

2

The Question of Capital Punishment

CAPITAL PUNISHMENT, like so many controversial subjects, has ramifications in many fields of thought and practice. Its implications reach into the fields of penology, sociology, law, justice, but above all, theology. Anything that touches life and death is, after all, theological, and any meaningful discussion must be so oriented. Indeed, one's theological viewpoint (or, more broadly, his philosophical orientation) will slant, if not settle, his attitude toward such a matter as capital punishment.

Capital punishment is defined as "the death penalty for crime." The concept includes the ideas that a crime has been committed, and thus the person executed is guilty. It also assumes that the government that carries out the sentence has been duly constituted (though the form of that government may vary). The specific crimes to which capital punishment applies cannot be stated in a definition, for this is really a separate question. The only matter before us is whether or not the principle of capital punishment is authorized by the Scripture.

This chapter, with minor changes, is reprinted from Charles C. Ryrie, "The Doctrine of Capital Punishment," *Bibliotheca Sacra* 129 (July-Sept. 1972): 211-17. Used by permission.

THE CURRENT DEBATE

The arguments advanced today against the legitimacy of capital punishment are usually along these lines: capital punishment cannot be harmonized with the love of God. The Christian gospel seeks the redemption of evildoers, which is the exact opposite of all that is involved in capital punishment. Jesus, we are told, "always recommended life and forgiveness over death and condemnation."[1] This is, generally speaking, a view that is an outworking of liberal theology which conveniently ignores Jesus' teaching about condemnation (Mt 5:21-26; 10:28; 12:32). It is often related to a societal redemption, rather than an individual redemption.

However, it is true that evangelicals are sometimes opposed to capital punishment for reasons unrelated to theology, such as the alleged impossibility of administering the matter fairly.[2]

Humanitarianism and the dignity and worth of society are other bases for decrying capital punishment. Albert Camus asks for sympathy to be shown for the family of the victim of capital punishment, stating that the death penalty strikes at the innocent (i.e., the family of the criminal). Ramsay Clark, while he was deputy attorney general of the United States, stated that "this nation is so great in its resources and too good in its purposes to engage in the light of recent understanding in the deliberate taking of human life as either a punishment or a deterrent to domestic crime."[3]

Coupled with these arguments is the continuous debate on the question of whether or not capital punishment is a deterrent to crime.[4] Perhaps the arguments against capital punishment (especially in a religious context) are best summarized in a resolution adopted in 1958 by the American Baptist Convention. It said.

1. *Because* human agencies and legal justice are fallible, and innocent men have been put to death, and

2. *Because* the Christian believes in the inherently sacred quality of all life as a gift of God, and

3. *Because* the deterrent effects of capital punishment are not clearly supported by the available evidence, and

4. *Because* the emphasis in modern penology is upon the process of creative, redemptive rehabilitation, rather than primitive retribution, we therefore

5. *Recommend* the abolition of capital punishment in those states which still practice it.[5]

On the other hand, many still argue for capital punishment. Five reasons for saying that the opposition to capital punishment is not for the common good are that such opposition "sides with evil; shows more regard for the criminal than the victim of the crime; weakens justice and encourages murder; is not based on Scripture but on a vague philosophical system that makes a fetish of the idea that the taking of life is wrong, under every circumstance, and fails to distinguish adequately between killing and murder, between punishment and crime."[6] In this statement the author has touched the heart of the issue: what does the Scripture teach? One's ethics are always based on one's philosophy or theology, which is ultimately related to one's view of the authority of the Bible. Although there can be honest difference of opinion between those who hold to the authority of the Bible, there can be no true light on any subject without trying to discover what the Bible says; and this is certainly true of the issue of capital punishment.

The Teaching of Scripture

Genesis 9:6. That this verse established the principle of capital punishment is in itself not debated. Murder is clearly to be punished by death because of the sanctity of human life. The foundation for this drastic punishment is the fact that man was made in the image of God; therefore, when violence in the form of murder is done to a man, it is in effect an outrage against God. How punishment is to be carried out is stated to be "by man"—thus leaving some flexibility as to the actual instrumentality of punishment. But that the principle extends to the entire race seems apparent from the simple fact that Noah, to whom it was given, stood at the head of a new beginning of the human race. What was given to Noah (such as the permission to eat meat and the promise of no further flood) was not confined to any race or family or cult.

The Mosaic law. The death penalty was also incorporated into the Mosaic code with a very significant difference. Whereas Genesis 9:6 only sanctions it in cases of murder, the Mosaic code required it for other offenses. The list was: murder (Ex 21:12; Num 35:16-31), working on the Sabbath (Ex 35:2), cursing father or mother (Lev 20:9), adultery (Lev 20:10), incest (Lev 20:11-12), sodomy (Lev 20:13, 15-16), false prophesying (Deu 13:1-10; 18: 20), idolatry (Deu 17:2-7), incorrigible juvenile delinquency (Deu 21:18-21), rape (Deu 22:25), keeping an ox that had killed a human being (Ex 21:29), kidnapping (Ex 21:16), and intrusion of an alien into a sacred place or office (Num 1:51; 3:10, 38; 17:7). The manner of execution (such as stoning or burning) is sometimes mentioned; where it is not indicated, one is left entirely to conjecture as to what was used.

John 8:1-11. Although there is a problem concerning the genuineness of this passage as a part of the true text of Scripture, most scholars agree that this records a true incident in the life of Christ, and it is often used by opponents of capital punishment as indicating His abolition of it. Certain facts seem to be clear in the passage. First, the motive of the scribes and Pharisees was to tempt Christ, to try to get a legal basis on which to accuse Him (v. 6). If he condoned the stoning, then He would have opened Himself to the charge of counseling action contrary to Roman law; and if He advised against stoning, He would have stood against the Mosaic law (Lev 20:10; Deu 22:22). Second, the Lord's answer not only extricated Him but raised the important point of the competency of the witnesses and accusers. If they, for instance, had not given the woman a warning, then she could not be convicted on their evidence. "No one, however factually guilty, can be lawfully convicted and executed on the evidence of incompetent witnesses. They would be 'joining with the wicked' if they allowed her, for all her adultery, to be a victim of injustice. The witnesses, and the elders, are put on their guard."[7] Third, Jesus did not reject the Mosaic law, for He enjoined that a stone be thrown (v. 7) This is no abolition of the death penalty!

Romans 13:1-7. Several important principles are established or reaffirmed in this passage: (1) human government is ordained by God (v. 1), yet it is a sphere of authority that is distinct from others like that of the home or the church; (2) human government is to be obeyed by the

Christian because it is of God, because it opposes evil (v. 4), and because our consciences tell us to obey (v. 5); (3) the government has the right of taxation (vv. 6-7); and (4) the government has the right to use force (v. 4), and this, of course, is the principle which impinges on our subject. The question is: what is included in its right to "bear the sword"?

Some understand that the sword does mean the authority of government to practice capital punishment, but they negate that authority on the basis of phrases which precede and follow in the context, such as "recompense to no man evil for evil" (12:17), "avenge not yourselves" (12:19), and "love worketh no ill to his neighbor" (13:10).[8] The exegetical difficulty with doing this is simply that it fails to recognize that these exhortations are directed to the individual in relation to his responsibility to other individuals within the body of Christ, while the teaching concerning the government's bearing the sword is in an entirely different context of group action and responsibility.

Others feel that the sword does not necessarily include capital punishment in its representation. It may, for instance, simply mean a policeman's pistol, and though it means that a governmental officer can bear arms, a court probably has no right to pass the death penalty.[9]

Others unhesitatingly state that "the sword is the symbol of the Magistrate's power to put to death."[10] While it is true that "the sword" may also include other rightful restraints in the proper function of government, such as fines, imprisonment, confiscation of property, it clearly includes execution of the death penalty. The word *sword* is significant, for the term, as explained by F. L. Godet, "Denotes (in opposition to . . . the poniard or straightedge sword) a large knife with bent blade, like that carried by the chiefs in the *Iliad*, and with which they cut the neck of the victims, similar to our *sabre*. By this expression, Paul does not here denote the weapon which the emperor and his pretorian prefect carried as a sign of their power of life and death—the application would be too restricted—but that which was worn at their side, in the provinces, by the superior magistrates, to whom belonged the right of capital punishment, and which they caused to be born solemnly before them in public processions."[11]

Godet goes on to point out, as have others, that it is impossible to exclude from the *right* of punishing the *kind* of punishment which the emblem (the sword) represents. If this verse only teaches the right of capital punishment without the practice of it, then presumably taxation, mentioned in the following verses, is only a symbol of the authority and does not refer to the actual taking of money from people. That, of course, is an impossible interpretation. Likewise, it is inconceivable to consider this verse as teaching only the government's right to use capital punishment without the actual exercise of that right.

In summary, it may be said that Romans 13:4 does teach the right of government to take the life of a criminal, although in what cases is not specified. The prerogative of capital punishment, established in Genesis 9:6, elaborated in the Mosaic code, not done away with in the teaching of Jesus, is affirmed in the doctrinal portion of the New Testament.

SOME QUESTIONS

A biblical question. Does the sixth commandment, "Thou shalt not kill" (Ex 20:13), abrogate the principle of capital punishment? The verb used in this verse occurs forty-nine times in the Old Testament and in every relevant use means "to murder," especially with premeditation. It is never used of animals, God, angels, or enemies in battle.*

The New Testament always translates the sixth commandment with *phoneuō* which is never used in any other sense than "to murder." The penalty for breaking the commandment was death (Ex 21:12; Num 35:16-21). One can conclude that when the theocracy took the life of a murderer (i.e., one who violated this sixth commandment), the state (and particularly those who actually performed the execution) was not guilty of murder. Furthermore, God's commanding Israel to kill their enemies during the conquest of Canaan could not have been a violation of this commandment either by God or by the individual soldiers who killed in battle. They were the instruments of the execution of divine judgment and not violators of the sixth commandment.

A theological question. Does an approach to the Scriptures that recognizes the progress of revelation or dispensational distinctions forbid the use of Genesis 9:6 as a guideline for today? There are only two ways that the answer could be yes. One is if in the progress of revelation, the New Testament declares a new ethic which replaces the Old Testament ethic which included capital punishment. But we have already seen that neither the Lord nor the apostles introduced a replacement ethic for capital punish-

---

*Of the 49 occurrences 36 are in the Pentateuch and Joshua related to laws regarding murder and manslaughter. Of the remaining 13, 2 involve an abstract use in the nominal form (Ps 42:10; Eze 21:22), 2 are quotations of the command (Jer 7:9; Ho 4:2), and the remainder mean murder.

ment; indeed, they did not disturb the Old Testament standard concerning this matter (Jn 8:1-11; Ro 13:1-7).

The other way would be to understand that the ending of the law in the New Testament carried with it the end of capital punishment which was an integral part of the law. Dispensationalists are strong in their insistence that the law has been done away with in Christ (2 Co 3:7-11). This, of course, would mean that the capital punishment *that was a part of the Mosaic law* was superseded by the law of grace, but by no stretch of any dispensational imagination could this include Genesis 9:6. Dispensational distinctions do recognize that the law of capital punishment for certain crimes was done away with in Christ, but this does not include capital punishment for murder. If the New Testament gave a replacement for the standard of Genesis 9:6, then it would no longer be valid. But since it does not, then the dispensational teaching concerning the end of the law is irrelevant to Genesis 9:6, and the principle of that verse apparently still applies today.

A practical question. What, after all, is the purpose of capital punishment? Numerous answers have been given and debated, but ultimately the biblical purpose is related to the responsibilities of civil government. It is the purpose of government to punish those who do evil (2 Pe 2:13), and capital punishment is evidently one of the ways this purpose is to be carried out. This raises the question of whether or not capital punishment is really a deterrent to crime. This question has been debated as far back as the fourth century before Christ in the governing assembly of Athens. The proponent of capital punishment argued that "any pity you show will win you no gratitude, but will be taken as a sign of weakness, and others will rebel if they see that it is possible to rebel with impunity." The opponent exhorted the assembly not to "do something foolish by trusting to the death penalty."

The argument continues today, and experts are cited on both sides of the question. J. Edgar Hoover's experienced appraisal was: "The professional law enforcement officer is convinced from experience that the hardened criminal has been and is deterred from killing based on the prospect of the death penalty."[12]

Recent experience in Great Britain indicates that the death penalty is a deterrent to crime. "There has been a sharp rise in armed robberies and violent crime throughout Britain since 1965, when the death penalty was dropped, and more criminals seem to carry guns now."[13]

In light of this evidence, at least, capital punishment does serve a purpose which is necessary to government carrying out its God-ordained function. Without it the sword of government would be sheathed.

3

The Question of Women's Lib

THE SECOND HALF of the twentieth century has seen greatly increased activity among women's liberation movements, both inside and outside the church. The advisability of a woman candidate for vice-president was given serious consideration in the national campaign of 1972 because of women's lib pressure. Equal pay for equal work is a goal which is being realized. Even the telephone company now has male operators (which is not uncommon in other countries) and repair women.

A generation ago some of the more liberal church groups began ordaining women ministers. Of more recent years some conservative denominations have followed suit. Usually there is a major discussion (and even battle) when the first woman is ordained; after that, the matter is accepted as not abnormal.

Of course, not all women's lib activities are necessarily bad. The Christian should be glad when any oppression is alleviated, and women's lib has done this in some areas (such as equal pay). The Bible does not give clear guidelines in all the secular areas in which women's lib works, though in some it does. For example, Paul's word in 1 Timothy 2:12-14 concerning Eve's being deceived may imply a deceivableness in the character of women which not only excludes them from leadership in the church but also in secular life, such as in political life. Clearly, the idea of removing children from their parents to communal centers is contrary to biblical teaching on the primacy of the home. The degrading of marriage as a desirable state is certainly contrary to the teaching of Scripture.

It is inevitable that the ideas and spirit of the secular aspects of women's lib should spill over into the church. Should women be ordained? Are deaconesses permitted by the Bible? What ministry can a woman have in the local church? These and similar questions are primary concerns about which the Christian must think in these days.

What Christianity Did for Women

Christianity was a women's lib movement long before current groups ever devised a plan. To understand just what Christianity did for women, one needs to know something of their status at the time of our Lord's coming to earth.

Women in Greek culture. Although Greek women were accorded somewhat higher respect than women of other ancient pagan societies, they were placed almost on the same level with slaves and were under the control of their husbands by custom and by law. The honor of wives was jealously guarded, though most of their time was spent in confinement at home. Demosthenes' summary is brutally frank: "*Hetairai* we keep for the sake of pleasure, concubines for the ordinary requirements of the body, wives to bear us legitimate children and to be faithful guardians of our households."[1]

It was only in Macedonia at the time of Christ that a minority of Greek women enjoyed a greater measure of freedom than women of other societies. That may account for the special mention made of them in relation to Paul's ministry in Thessalonica (Ac 17:4). But all in all, women were considered as decidedly inferior to men.

Women in Roman society. Women enjoyed greater practical, if not legal, freedom in Roman society than in Greek. With this partial emancipation came increased moral laxity, including more frequent divorce. The relatively few who followed the teachings of the Stoics did elevate the position of women and sought to live by a high ethical standard. Roman religions often incorporated shameful vices which greatly degraded women. In the Roman world just before the coming of Christ, "almost every vice was rampant—immorality and paiderastia, abortion and infanticide, gluttony and avarice, cruelty and sycophancy, gambling and suicide, indecency in pictures, at public races, and on the stage."[2] And yet, like today, in the midst of a corrupt society there were many among the common people who had neither part nor lot in these practices.

Women in Judaism. A woman's position in Judaism seems to be a paradox which can only be solved by recognizing the distinction made between her proper and improper spheres of service. In the home her position was one of dignity and responsibility (Pr 31). Children were the special charge of the mother (Ex 20:12; 21:15; Lev 19:3). Legally her position was low, but practically she occupied a more dignified position. The right of divorce was at the discretion of the husband, and, when exercised, all that the wife could expect was a bill of divorcement.

Though women took part in religious activities (Deu 12:12, 18; 14:26; 16:11, 14), "the majority [of women] were entirely dependent on men, and became in religious

matters a sort of appendix to their husbands, who by their
good actions insured salvation also for them."[3] The law
expected the presence of women at the sanctuary at the
festal seasons, and they were permitted to share in eating
all the offerings except the sin offering (Lev 6:29; 10:14).
Yet there is no question but that men dominated the religious scene in Judaism. The major contribution of Jewish women was in their service in the home where they
were accorded a place of honor in carrying out the privileges of motherhood.

   Women in the time of Christ. Jesus Christ introduced a
new appraisal of women. He offered them spiritual privileges equal to those given to men, but He did not sanction
equal spiritual activities. A band of women ministered to
Jesus of their material wealth (Lk 8:2-3), and He received
their ministrations (Lk 10:38-42; 23:56; Jn 4:6-42). In
His parables He frequently included references to women's
everyday lives (Mt 13:33; Lk 15:8-9). Women were the
first to receive the news of the resurrection. The Lord
opened the privileges of religious faith equally to women
as well as to men. We must conclude that as regards spiritual privileges, Jesus considered the two sexes equal.

   But as regards spiritual activity, the Lord recognized a
difference. What Christ did not say about women is as
important as what He did say. It is significant that no
woman was chosen to be among the twelve disciples. The
Lord's Supper was instituted in the presence of men only.
The apostolic commissions of John 20:19-23 and Matthew
28:16-20 were given to men only (though the Spirit fell
on women as well as men on the day of Pentecost). Paul
did not include the mention of any woman in the list of
witnesses of the resurrection in 1 Corinthians 15 though

women did witness it. And, of course, the incarnation itself was in a man. "Jesus is not the radical reformer who proclaims laws and seeks to enforce a transformation of relationships. He is the Saviour who gives Himself especially to the lowly and oppressed and calls all without distinction to the freedom of the kingdom of God."[4]

What Women Did for Christianity

The founding of the church. When the Holy Spirit descended at Pentecost there were women among the 120 disciples gathered in the upper room. But the preaching was done by a man, Peter. The question of Peter's use of Joel 2 is a very complex one and is not solved by the oversimplified conclusion that Peter said it was fulfilled by the church. It would be risky at best to conclude the validity of women preachers today from the fact that Peter said that "your sons and your daughters shall prophesy." If prophesying by both sexes is to be characteristic of the church, then so should be the other things in the passage like "blood, and fire, and vapour of smoke, . . . the sun . . . turned into darkness, and the moon into blood" (Ac 2:19-20).

Women often served as hostesses for the churches which in those early days met in homes. Mary, the mother of John Mark, apparently opened her home as a meeting place in Jerusalem (Ac 12:12), and some suggest that Euodias and Syntyche acted as hostesses for house churches in Philippi (Phil 4:2). When the Christian message first went into Europe, the earliest converts were women (Lydia at Philippi, "honorable women" at Thessalonica and Berea, and Damaris at Athens, Ac 16:14; 17:4, 12, 34). At Corinth, Priscilla and Phebe were active in the work of the church though the exact nature of their activities is unclear (Ac 18:26; Ro 16:1-3).

In various ways, women served the new churches but apparently always in a secondary place. The apostles were all men. The missionary activity was done by men. The writing of the New Testament was the work of men. The leadership of the churches was in the hands of men. Equality of spiritual position for women did not mean equality of spiritual ministry.

Galatians 3:28. "There is neither Jew nor Greek, there is neither bond nor free, there is neither male nor female: for ye are all one in Christ Jesus." This verse, often misused by women's libbers and others, does not say that either the distinctions or the limitations of sex are erased in Christ. If it were teaching that, it would also have to be understood to be saying that the slave—master difference was erased among believers. But Paul never quoted this verse when writing later to Philemon about his slave Onesimus. The "no difference" between bond and free did not mean that Onesimus was set free from his Christian master. The "no difference'" between Jew and Greek did not mean that after Paul became a believer he was no longer a Jew (2 Co 11:22; Ro 11:1). The "no difference" between male and female means no difference in spiritual privilege, not spiritual activity. It does not mean that women should do men's jobs in the church any more than it means that men should do women's jobs in the home.

Restrictions on the ministry of women. The activities of women were primarily connected with the home (1 Ti 5:14; Titus 2:4-5), and the epistles restrict their public ministry. Before examining these restrictions, one matter needs to be clarified. Prophesying and preaching are not synonymous; therefore, the fact that women did prophesy does not give sanction to women preaching today (Ac 21: 9). The prophet delivered a message which came directly from God as an objective matter. The preacher or teacher, by contrast, becomes subjectively involved in the objectively given message (now written in the Bible) and then delivers the result. Furthermore, the gift of prophet is always distinguished in the New Testament from the gifts of pastor and teacher (Ro 12:6-7; 1 Co 12:29; Eph 4:11). They are not the same gifts. The reference in 1 Corinthians 14:3 is a description of the results of the exercise of the gift of prophecy; it is not a definition of the gift. If prophesying and preaching were the same, there would be no need to make these careful distinctions in the New Testament.

In 1 Corinthians 11:5 Paul wrote: "But every woman that prayeth or prophesieth with her head uncovered dishonoureth her head: for that is even all one as if she were shaven." Later in the same epistle (14:34) he said: "Let your women keep silence in the churches: for it is not permitted unto them to speak; but they are commanded to be under obedience, as also saith the law." In the former reference, Paul seems to imply that women may pray and prophesy in public if veiled. Yet when he discusses the subject of the exercise of spiritual gifts, he apparently withdraws that limited permission. In 1 Timothy 2:12 he is equally emphatic in declaring that women are not to teach in the church.

Several solutions have been offered to this apparent contradiction:

1. Some say that Paul withdrew the permission for women to speak, upon further reflection. Of course, such a view denies verbal inspiration.

2. Others say that 1 Corinthians 14:34 refers to hysterical outbursts or calling back and forth and does not prohibit orderly preaching by women. The verb "to speak" is made to mean "to chatter"; however, it is the common word for speak and Paul uses it in the same epistle of his own preaching (2:13).

3. Others believe that the command to be silent was that which was being said by some in the congregation, but was not Paul's command. This seems to be a highly artificial way of viewing chapter 14, which is clearly Paul's reply to them, not their questions or reports to him. It is also said that 1 Timothy 2:12 is a prohibition only if a qualified man is available to teach. But the verse literally says, "I do not permit a woman to be a teacher, nor must woman domineer over man; she should be quiet" (NEB). Possible domination is the reason women are not to be teachers. The verse does not say that women are forbidden to teach only when they might usurp authority. Neither does the verse say that a woman may never teach. It says that women are not to become teachers. The tense of the infinitive is present, indicating that the continuous exercise of teaching is what is forbidden.

The only solution to this apparent contradiction is to be found by observing Paul's own emphasis in the contexts of these passages in order to discover which passage would guide the interpretation of the other. Those who wish to give women a place of ministry in the church emphasize 1 Corinthians 11, and those who wish to restrict their ministry capitalize on chapter 14. Which should govern the other? The context can help us decide.

The subject of chapter 11 is the sign of the subordination of women. The subject of chapter 14 is the exercise of spiritual gifts in the church. Therefore, we should expect to find the instruction concerning the ministry of women in the church in chapter 14, and that instruction is that they should keep silent. What then does Paul mean when he seems to recognize that women prophesied (11:5)? He does admit that some women in Corinth were doing this, but it does not follow that he approved of it. This is the very important point that is overlooked. When he does come to the place in the epistle where he speaks his mind on the subject, he lays down a strict prohibition against women speaking at all in the church. Perhaps one might justify a woman speaking on rare occasion from 11:5 and even possibly from the present tense of "to teach" in 1 Timothy 2: 12, but such, if it is justified, is exceptional and unusual. And such exceptions scarcely justify or even imply the ordination of women to a regular ministry. Robertson and Plummer summarize the matter with balance. Concerning the women at Corinth they say:

> They had been claiming equality with men in the matter of the veil, by discarding this mark of subjection in Church, and apparently they had also been attempting to preach, or at any rate had been asking questions during service. We are not sure whether St. Paul contemplated the *possibility* of women prophesying in exceptional cases. What is said in xi. 5 may be hypothetical. Teaching he forbids them to attempt.[5]

The sense of these three passages reveals that the early church did not countenance the practice of permitting women to speak in their public meetings. Perhaps a woman gave an occasional prophecy, but such was decidedly the exception and was not the exercise of the gifts of pastor or teacher. In any case, no woman was to assume the office of a teacher or pastor. The scriptural ideal is that women should not lead in any way in public worship. Today, however, the matter is complicated by the fact that we have many more services than the early church did. Does the prohibition apply to all these added services? Cannot a woman teach a Sunday school class of nonadults (where there is no possibility of usurping the authority of the man)? Why should she also not be permitted to teach adult women or pray in a women's prayer meeting? Apparently even such activities as these must never interfere with her responsibilities in her home and with her own children, which have top priority.

Of course, we do not live in an ideal world. There are many occasions at home and abroad when there are no men to do the work. In such cases women have had to do what is not expected that they should do. When this happens, the woman who finds herself doing a man's job should so plan her work that a man could take it over as soon as possible. The acid test any woman can apply to such situations is this: would she be willing and anxious to give over her work to a qualified man if he should appear on the scene at any time?

Women in places of leadership. The leaders of the New Testament churches were elders and deacons, and it is clear that only men could qualify for these positions (see 1 Ti 3:2, 12). The only possible place of leadership for a woman might have been as a deaconess. Two passages in the epistles are used to support the existence of the office of deaconess (1 Ti 3:11; Ro 16:1-2). However, neither passage furnishes clear evidence. The women referred to in the former passage are wives of the deacons and accompanied them in their ministrations, especially in the homes of widows. If these women were officially recognized deaconesses, one would expect verse 11 to follow verse 13 so that Paul would have completed what he had to say about deacons before beginning on deaconesses. The fact that verse 11 appears within the verses specifying qualifications for deacons indicates that these were the deacons' wives. In Romans 16:1 Phebe is designated a *diakonon* (servant) of the church in Cenchrea. This scarcely implies an official order of deaconesses to which she belonged (in that case one would expect a feminine article with the noun or the feminine word *diakonissa*). Historically, deaconesses are not seen as a recognized order until the third century, and they likely arose out of the widows of the church. Women were not involved in the leadership responsibilities of the early church.

To sum up: (1) the primary and honored place of the Christian woman is in her home, which takes precedence over all other opportunities; (2) her position in the body of Christ is equal to that of every other believer; (3) her function as far as office and activity is restricted, recognizing the leadership and ministry of the church as the responsibility of men.

This leads to a final and very important consideration: the subject of the role of women in the church from whatever viewpoint and with whatever conclusions should never be discussed alone. It ought always to be considered in relation to the scriptural teaching concerning the role of men in the church. If women are out of place, the reason is usually that men are not assuming their God-appointed place. If men were responding to the call to vocational Christian service, the question of the ordination of women might not arise. If men were going to the mission fields, the problem of women doing men's work on those fields would never come up. If men knew the Scriptures and were zealous to teach the Word, there would be enough men teachers to do the job. If men would qualify themselves and respond to the opportunities to serve on the governing boards of our churches, there would be no lack of leadership. Men in their proper role would solve many of the practical problems concerning the role of women.

4

The Question of Divorce

AN ATTORNEY FRIEND of mine told me that invariably the first question a client asks him in a divorce action is this: "Do you think I'll win?" To this question, he said, his standard reply is simply, "Of course not. In a divorce nobody wins."

The United States Census Bureau reports that in 1920 there was one divorce for every seven marriages; in 1940, one divorce for every six marriages; in 1960, one divorce for every four marriages; and in 1972 one divorce for every three marriages. Of course, many of these divorces involve Christians who in turn involve pastors and churches in different situations and decisions. Too, in many cases remarriage enters the picture, and this further complicates matters. The Bible has a good deal to say on these subjects, though what it does say is directed to those who are in the family of God, not outside it.

THE QUESTION OF DIVORCE

The Teaching of the Old Testament. God's original design for man was one wife and no separation (Gen 2:23-24; Mt 19:6). And yet the Mosaic law did permit or tolerate divorce (Deu 24:1-4). Actually this passage does not approve of divorce. Rather, it states that when certain things

45

happen (those mentioned in vv. 1-3), a certain prohibition follows (v. 4). In other words, verses 1-3 state the
condition and verse 4 the conclusion. What this passage
particularly teaches is the prohibition of taking back a
wife who has been divorced from her first husband, has
married another man and then has been freed from him
either by death or a second divorce. In such cases, the first
husband was forbidden to take his former wife back. In
stating the law, Moses acknowledges that a bill of divorce
was sometimes given, but the law did not institute it or
sanction it.

The reason a man might divorce his wife is stated as
"some uncleanness in her," and this phrase has been the
subject of much discussion. It cannot mean adultery, for
the penalty for that was death (Lev 20:10; Deu 22:22).
Nor can it mean adultery suspected but not proven, for
there was a test for this (Num 5:11-31). The words suggest some repulsive or immodest exposure (see Deu 23:
14), but the phrase is so indefinite as to give rise to con-
troversy in the Rabbinic schools at the time of Christ; the
school of Shammai understanding by it unchastity and that
of Hillel any physical blemish or even a trivial cause of dis-
like. The more lenient view of Hillel enjoyed greater
popularity and was usually followed.

The Lord Jesus affirmed the fact that the law did not
sanction divorce but only permitted it (Mt 19:3-9). When
the Pharisees asked Him if it was lawful to divorce "for
every cause" (v. 3), they were trying either to force the
Lord to support a lower moral standard than He should or
to support the strict interpretation which would make Him
unpopular. It was assumed that a man had the right to
divorce his wife; the only question was, On what ground?

Divorces were granted because a woman merely broke a single part of the Mosaic law, or when the behavior of a woman was such as to put her husband in a bad light, or because of barrenness, or if illness or the occupation of the husband was such as to make continued living with him unthinkable.[1] The Lord, however, took His questioners back to the original institution of marriage and showed that the bond was intended to be indissoluble. Divorce under the Mosaic law was allowed only because of the hardness of the hearts of the people.

At the close of the Old Testament period, the prophet Malachi condemned the increasing divorce rate among the people (Mal 2:13-16). God's attitude toward divorce is stated in no uncertain terms: "For the Lord, the God of Israel, saith that he hateth putting away" (v. 16; see Deu 22:19, 29 for the same word *putting away* which means ("divorce"). One of the reasons given is that divorce is contrary to God's original purpose for marriage; that is, one man and one woman joined together to become one flesh (Mal 2:15). Thus, from this passage, too, we are forced to conclude that the Old Testament did not sanction divorce, although it prescribed what could not be done under a particular circumstance which involved divorce (Deu 24:1-4).

The Teaching of Christ. The Lord's teaching on this subject is contained in Matthew 5:31-32; 19:3-9; Mark 10:2-12; and Luke 16:18. The principal question raised by these passages is the apparent exception to what otherwise seems to be a complete prohibition against divorce. The exception, fornication, appears in both of the Matthew passages but not in Mark or Luke. This further complicates the question, since the Lord seems to be saying in one place that no divorce is the rule and in another that divorce is permitted in cases of fornication.

Several solutions to this problem have been proposed. They fall into two categories: those that understand fornication to be a legitimate reason for divorce and those that feel there is no legitimate cause for divorce.

Some understand that if fornication has occurred, then divorce is permitted. John Murray says:

> We are compelled to take the position that if the exceptive clause belongs to Matthew's Gospel, then it truly represents our Lord's teaching. It would be incompatible with the inspiration of Scripture to reject Matthew in favour of Mark and Luke, as it would also be to reject Mark and Luke in favour of Matthew. . . . In such a case the accounts in Matthew would simply affirm that there is one exception to the rule that whoever puts away his wife causes her to commit adultery, namely, antecedent adultery on the part of the wife herself.[2]

And, in another place, the same author states: "The one exception . . . underlies the illegitimacy of any other reason."[3]

A refinement of this view states that the husband (H) would have to divorce his wife (W) if she had committed adultery with someone (A), since not to do so would involve him in an adulterous act with a woman who had become one flesh with someone else (HWA). The husband's only option would be to continue to live with his wife in total abstinence.[4]

A second view is that divorce is permitted when unfaithfulness occurs during the period of betrothal. In other words, fornication is unfaithfulness during the betrothal period. If it occurs then, the engagement must be broken, and this could be done only by a bill of divorce. During Jesus' time the custom was as follows:

> At the betrothal, the bridegroom, personally or by deputy, handed to the bride a piece of money or a letter, it being expressly stated in each case that the man thereby espoused the woman. From the moment of betrothal both parties were regarded, and treated in law (as to inheritance, adultery, need of formal divorce) as if they had been actually married, except as regarded their living together.[5]

This concept of divorce as meaning the breaking of the engagement is seen in Joseph's dilemma when he discovered Mary to be pregnant. He "was minded to put her away privily" (Mt 1:19). In other words, he had decided (before the angel appeared to him and confirmed the truth of the conception by the Holy Spirit) to break the engagement, and the only way he could do that was by giving her a bill of divorce. He would have done it privately; that is, in the presence of two witnesses only. If this be the meaning of the exception clause in the Lord's teaching, then we would have to say that today it sanctions the breaking of an engagement if one party has been unfaithful during that period, but that the teaching does not permit divorce after marriage.

A third view, held by those who do not accept the inspiration of the text, states that the Lord's true teaching disallowed for divorce in every instance, and that the exception clause in Matthew is in reality not a part of the genuine teaching of Christ but a gloss added later. George Salmon says:

> It seems to me that St. Mark's version, which appears to

disallow divorce without any exception, is more likely
to represent the common source than St. Matthew's,
which excepts the case of the adulterous wife. For it is
much easier to account for St. Matthew's insertion of the
words than for St. Mark's omission of them, if they had
been in the original.[6]

Such a view is unacceptable to those of us who accept the
integrity of all these texts.

The Roman Catholic church admits of no exception that
would permit divorce, and yet she is faced with the problem of making all the texts consistent. The solution proposed is "that explanation is at once found if we consider
that the words 'put away' in St. Matthew refer to separation only and not to dissolution."[7] However, this simply
is not the meaning of "put away;" it is only the dogma of
the church.

Finally, there is the viewpoint that understands fornication to have in these two passages in Matthew (not every-
where) a particular meaning; namely, marriage of too near
relatives as prohibited in Leviticus 18:6-18. In other words,
if this be the correct interpretation, the Lord taught that
divorce was not permitted unless there had been a marriage
of close relatives, in which case it was permitted. This is
most likely the meaning of fornication in Acts 15:29. W. K.
Lowther Clarke explains it this way:

> Since the first three articles of the compromise are con-
> cerned with practices innocent enough to the Gentiles,
> the fourth must be of a similar nature. . . . *Porneia* here
> means *marriage within the prohibited Levitical degrees.*
> . . . But for a decade or two, especially in places like Anti-
> och, where Jew and Gentile met and where the agitation
> which led to the decree arose, *marriage within the prohib-*

ited degrees was a live issue, and *porneia* was the word by which it was known. . . . One exception is allowed to the universal rule: when a man who has married within the prohibited degrees puts away his wife the word adultery is out of place. Rather the marriage is null. . . . There is no divorce, but cases of nullity may be recognized.[8]

Whether one concludes that fornication means unfaithfulness in marriage, unfaithfulness during betrothal, or marriage of near relatives, it is perfectly clear that the Lord did not allow for divorce for any other cause.

One final observation: the disciples understood the Lord's teaching to be very strict, for their reaction (even in Matthew's record where the exception appears) is, "If the case of the man be so with his wife, it is not good to marry" (Mt. 19:10). This seems to support the idea that He did not allow for divorce after marriage, for if He were saying that it was permitted for fornication, then His standard was not much higher than the school of Shammai, and that would hardly have provoked such a response from the disciples. One is driven to the conclusion that either the second or the final view is the correct interpretation of the exception clause, and that our Lord did not allow for divorce after marriage.

The Teaching of Paul. Paul seems to agree with this conclusion about Christ's teaching, for he taught no separation of believers (1 Co 7:10). If an unauthorized separation should occur, Paul offered two alternatives: the wife must remain unmarried permanently, or be reconciled to her husband (1 Co 7:11). In this teaching he claimed to be reflecting the doctrine of Christ, and he mentions no exceptions.

Paul also deals with certain cases about which the Lord

said nothing (this is the meaning of the phrase: "But to the rest speak I, not the Lord," v. 12). These are the cases of spiritually mixed marriages (one partner a believer and the other not). Again the rule is: no separation (1 Co 7:12-16). Jewish law required the unbeliever to be put away (Ezra 9:1–10:44), but the Christian should live with the unbelieving partner in order to have a witness in the home. This might lead to the conversion of the partner and the children. The presence of the believer does not guarantee the salvation of the others but does give a better opportunity to demonstrate the gospel in action. This is why the children of spiritually mixed parents are "holy," that is, set apart in a way that children of unbelieving parents are not. Again, divorce is not permitted; the marriage union should be preserved at all costs.

To sum up: our Lord apparently taught the indissolubility of marriage as the norm. Marriage between near relatives may be annulled, or engagement may be broken because of unfaithfulness, but marriage is permanent. And this was the way God intended it to be from the beginning. The apostle Paul's teaching is the same; indeed, he adds the fact that there should not even be a separation short of divorce both in cases of believers and spiritually mixed marriages. This is not an easy conclusion to reach or teach, especially in a day of easy divorce, but it does seem to be the teaching of the Scriptures.

REMARRIAGE

If one favors the view that fornication is a legitimate cause for divorce, then it follows that remarriage is permitted to the innocent party on the basis of Matthew 19:9. "Innocent party" is a relative term, but what is meant is that the party who did not actually commit the act of adultery may remarry. If, on the other hand, the Lord's teaching is understood as forbidding divorce, then the question of remarriage would never arise.

However, the meaning of Paul's teaching in 1 Corinthians 7:15 is debated in this connection: "But if the unbelieving depart, let him depart. A brother or a sister is not under bondage in such cases: but God hath called us to peace." Some understand this to mean that if the believer is deserted by the unbelieving partner, he or she is free to remarry. This is supported by the fact that the verb "depart" in the middle voice (as it is in this verse) was almost a technical term for divorce in the papyri.[9] That it is so used in this verse is very doubtful.

Others understand Paul to be saying that if the unbelieving partner leaves, the believer is not bound to go beyond reasonable measures to prevent it. To continue to be bound would be slavery. Divorce is forbidden, but dismissal may have to be accepted by the believing partner in a spiritually mixed marriage. And this verse is dealing only with such mixed cases.

Remarriage is, of course, clearly permitted in the case of those who have lost their partners through death. In this same chapter Paul recognizes this as long as the marriage is with a believer (v. 39, "only in the Lord"). In a similar vein he suggests that young widows marry (1 Ti 5:14).

To sum up: some feel that the innocent party in an adultery case may remarry without question, and that the deserted believer in a spiritually mixed marriage may remarry, as well as the widow or widower. Others feel that only the widow or widower is free to remarry. The stricter view seems to be the clearer teaching of Scripture.

SOME PRACTICAL CONSIDERATIONS

One of the questions frequently asked is this: If a divorce and remarriage occur before one is saved, does this change matters? Is not the slate wiped clean at the time of salvation so that any divorce or remarriage does not affect the future of the parties involved? Reasoning like this fails to take into account two important considerations. First, while it is absolutely true that at the time of salvation the guilt of sin is entirely forgiven, it is not true that the history of one's past and its effects are erased. The criminal saved in jail does not gain an automatic release or a wiping clean of his record. Sometimes the most dedicated missionary candidate is barred from the country of his calling by a police record in his home country which will stop the issuance of a visa by the foreign country. The police record need be only one small charge against him, and it makes no difference whether the incident took place before or after he was saved.

Another important fact that must be considered in this question is that the underlying basis of marriage is the concept of "one flesh." To be sure, becoming one flesh does not make a marriage in all cases, just as, in some cases, marriage does not result in becoming one flesh. Nevertheless, there is no sexual intercourse that does not make one flesh (notice 1 Co 6:16). This concept definitely underlies the Lord's teaching concerning divorce, and it is, at least in part, the basis for Paul's counsel to the couple to stay together. The salvation of a couple or of one of the partners does not in any way change the fact that they were made one flesh at the time of marriage. If that union was broken by divorce, the guilt of sin is forgiven at salvation, though the facts of history cannot be altered.

A second question is this: what is the meaning of the phrase "husband of one wife" (1 Ti 3:2, 12; Titus 1:6), and how does it relate to this discussion? There is much disagreement as to the meaning of this phrase, but the viewpoints boil down to two basic ones: it is a prohibition against bigamy and polygamy (more than one wife at the same time), or it forbids digamy (being married twice legally). The former is, of course, a much easier interpretation to follow, but it seems an unnecessary prohibition since polygamy was not practiced by the Greeks and Romans. It is more difficult to consider this a prohibition against a second marriage after the death of the first wife, and yet this seems to be what Paul is saying. The same kind of phrase is used in 1 Timothy 5:9 where it clearly means that the enrolled widow shall have been married only once. The only objection against the view that this prohibits digamy is the fact that Paul elsewhere allows for a second marriage after the death of the first spouse (1 Co 7:9). However, this is not a contradiction, since the prohibition in 1 Timothy is in relation to the elders and deacons, whereas the permission in 1 Corinthians is for laity in general. In other words, there is really no contradiction since the restriction is applied only to a special group in the church. Leadership responsibilities do incur restriction on the liberty others may enjoy. Alan G. Nute says, "Perhaps he deemed it advisable to recommend to men responsible for setting an example of strict personal discipline, that they refrain from remarriage on the death of a partner."[10]

In summary, if "husband of one wife" means married only one time ever, then the remarriage of a man to a believer after the death of his first wife would disqualify him from serving as an elder or a deacon in the church.

A final question is this: Are there never any justifiable grounds for divorce? If by "justifiable" is meant scriptural, the answer seems to be no. Everything in the New Testament points to the disallowance of divorce. Marriage is placed on the most ideal plane, and the union is to be kept inviolate. However, believers do not always live according to God's ideal standards, and divorces do occur. Indeed, in some instances, it may seem as if a divorce is not only inevitable but desirable. Everything should be done to prevent the dissolution of a marriage. If it happens, then remarriage seems to be out of the question. Yet if divorce and/or remarriage do occur, this does not mean that God is through with those individuals. But it does mean certain restrictions in service, for the example of a divorced or remarried person is not that which should be held up to young people in the church. The church should receive such people and minister to their special needs and seek to help them find a proper place of usefulness.

An ounce of prevention is worth a pound of cure! Perhaps we are spending too much time today seeking to find the innocent party or determining a policy under which the pastor may marry divorced persons or considering where such persons may serve in the local church. These things should have their proper consideration, but it is far more important to indoctrinate young people in scriptural standards concerning marriage. The standard is: "what therefore God hath joined together, let not man put asunder" (Mt 19:6).

5

The Question of Race

FOR MANY REASONS racial questions continue to be an important area of discussion in our day. Civil rights agitation and legislation brought these matters before the minds of people who were never concerned about them before. Some churches have given sums of money to minority groups as penance for past sins. Public school integration and busing have brought the issue into almost every home. What does the Bible say about racial differences, and what should be the believer's attitude toward those of other races?

THE CURSE ON CANAAN (Gen 9:20-27)

Unfortunately, some Christians apparently still seem to feel that the Bible placed a curse on certain races which makes them inferior. This is based upon a misunderstanding of the curse placed on Canaan after the flood. Since this misconception still persists, it would be well to examine the account on which it is based.

The sin of Noah. Some time had elapsed after the flood, for Noah's son Ham already had children, and Noah and his family had begun to rehabilitate the earth. Noah's planting a vineyard was apparently not the first time this had been done in the history of the world. The practice of agriculture was as old as Cain (Gen 4:2), and the excessive misuse of wine had probably been previously experienced by men. While the word *drinking* in Matthew 24:38 does not of itself necessarily imply drunkenness, the usual word for "eating" in that verse does give the picture of a pre-flood world filled with animal delights (since it is a word used of horses or mules eating). Noah's culpability is underscored by the fact that his was not the first case of drunkenness in the history of the world. The fact that this was the seasoned saint who had stood his ground against the whole world before the flood makes his sin all the more terrible.

Raising grapes led to making a drink from them, and the taste of the wine led to excess, and the excess led to stupor which made Noah want to lie down; then the warmth from the wine made him uncover himself (the verb in Genesis 9:21 is not passive "was uncovered" but reflexive "uncovered himself"), and the stage was fully set for the drama that followed.

In came Ham and saw his naked father. The verb *saw* means more than a harmless or accidental look. It indicated that Ham gazed with satisfaction at his father. Though there was no overt inordinate act on Ham's part with his father, his unclean thoughts were fed by gazing on his father, and, at the least, his act bespoke a complete lack of proper filial respect. He then went to tell his brothers what he had seen.

In contrast, Shem and Japheth went into their father's tent backward, so as not to see Noah's condition, and they covered his naked body. In this day of nudity in the world and casualness, disrespect, and insolence on the part of children toward their parents, these actions of Noah and his sons almost seem trivial, if not irrelevant. But God did not consider them so, for they indicated, then as now, something very wrong within the hearts of those involved.

The prophecy of Noah. When Noah woke up, he inquired ("knew," verse 24, means to find out by inquiring) what his younger son had done to him. Then he pronounced a blessing on Shem and Japheth and a curse, not on Ham, but on only one of Ham's four sons, Canaan (see 10:6). In this very point lies the mistake many people make concerning this prophecy. They think that the curse was placed on Ham and thereby on African people. The identifications of Ham's other sons are as follows: Cush—Ethiopia; Mizraim—Egypt; Phut—Libya. These were the progenitors of the tribes that populated Africa. However, anyone who stops and thinks a minute will recognize that Canaan was the father of those who occupied Phoenicia and Palestine, the Canaanites.

Canaan's sons (Gen 10:15-18) were Sidon (the inhabitants of the Phoenician city in Lebanon), Heth (the Hittites, Syria, Jos 1:4), Jebusites (dwellers in the hills around Jerusalem), Amorites (those who inhabited the hill country on both sides of the Jordan), Girgasites (inhabitants of Canaan, Gen 15:21), Hivites (early inhabitants of Syria and Palestine), Arkites (dwellers in Lebanon, 1 Ch 1:15), Sinites (inhabitants of the Lebanese coastal area), Arvadites (dwellers on an island off the coast of Syria, fifty miles north of Byblos), Zemarites, (those who lived in the territory of Benjamin), and the Hamathites (those who lived near the Orontes river). As you can see, none of these were inhabitants of Africa. The Canaanites were those wicked inhabitants of Palestine whom God commanded to be destroyed under Joshua because of their extreme wickedness. The subjugation of these people was the primary fulfillment of Noah's prediction of servitude. But because the Israelites failed to destroy them completely when they went into the land, the heathen religion of the Canaanites was embraced by the Israelites, resulting in the worship of a kind of Canaanized Yahweh. Phoenician religion also centered around Baal worship and fertility cults.

The Assyrians captured Phoenician cities in 842 B.C. After the fall of Assyria, the Babylonians controlled the territory, then the Persians, and then Alexander the Great who captured the territory in 332 B.C. Greek and Aramaic replaced the Phoenician language, and although the cities continued to be important until they fell to Moslem invaders in A.D. 600, as a distinctive people the Phoenicians were pretty well diluted by the time of the Roman conquest in 64 B.C.

Clearly the curse was placed on Canaan and not on Ham, but the question of why Canaan was singled out is difficult to answer. Some suggest that since Ham had already been blessed (Gen 9:1), he could not have been cursed by his father, thus the curse had to fall on Canaan. Others point out that although Canaan apparently had no direct involvement in Ham's actions, Ham's failure to respect his father was punished by his having a son who would dishonor him. In other words, Ham was punished in his son. Whatever the answer, the punishment is clear, and it was from God.

To summarize: the curse on Canaan was from God; it did not include Ham or three of his four sons (and therefore was not on the Negroes) ; it was deserved in its outworking because of the extreme wickedness of the Canaanites; and it is irrelevant today since it would be difficult, if not impossible, to identify a Canaanite.

THE NEW TESTAMENT ETHIC

Concerning impartiality. Several important passages in the New Testament relate the impartiality of God to ethnic issues. Peter recognized that today God sends the message of salvation through faith in Christ to all men, regardless of ethnic background (Ac 10:34-35). Thus the believer should be concerned about getting the gospel to all men without distinction of racial or national background. The New Testament also reminds us that the judgments of God are without partiality as well (Ro 2:11; 1 Pe 1:17). Also, employers are especially warned to treat their employees impartially (Eph 6:9; Col 3:25).

In the assembly partiality is outlawed (Ja 2:1-9). The particular problem in the early church which James deals with centered around preference being shown in the assembly to those who had money. They were given seats of honor, while poorer people were shunted to the rear. While the passage is speaking against partiality because of economic differences, it certainly applies to similar instances which might arise because of racial differences. To refuse to admit or to seat in an obscure place a person who comes into a church and who is of a different race than that which predominates in that church is to "have respect to persons" and thus to "commit sin" (v. 9).

The church at Antioch exemplified impartiality. The leaders of that church mentioned in Acts 13:1 were probably all Jewish believers. Simeon, one of them, had the nickname Niger, which is Latin for black. It may mean that he was a Jew of African origin or possibly that he was an African Gentile who was a proselyte to Judaism, but he shared equally in the leadership of the church with those of differing backgrounds.

To sum up: believers are to be impartial in their giving out the gospel, in employer—employee relationships, and in their acceptance into the church of all who come.

Concerning distinctions. Impartial actions do not necessarily mean similar actions toward everyone. The New Testament teaching also includes this principle of distinction. Unity and diversity need not be contradictory principles, and the New Testament insists on both within the body of Christ. The diversity of spiritual gifts is to work for the unity of individuals in the body who possess those gifts (Eph 4:11-13). Unity of position and possessions in Christ does not obliterate distinctions of nature or spheres of opportunity (Gal 3:28). That verse cannot mean that men and women cease to be distinct when they become Christians; nor does it mean that the Jewish and Gentile peoples are no longer recognizably distinct. Indeed, although Jews and Gentiles were members of and workers together in local assemblies, the fact that they are different people is still noted (1 Co 10:32; Gal 6:16). When differences in their backgrounds erupted in serious differences of opinions regarding Christian conduct, the early church sought to bring harmony between the races by suggesting regulations for conduct (Ac 15:19-20; 1 Co 9:20-21).

To sum up: distinctions, including racial distinctions, remain even after salvation. They do not affect spiritual possessions, but they may affect the kind of spiritual activity (as in the case of men and women) or the conduct of spiritual living (as in the case of those with different backgrounds).

Contemporary Problems and Practice

Christlikeness. For the Christian the pattern and goal of

his life and conduct is Christlikeness. What this means can best be understood by a continual reading and study of the gospels where He is portrayed and by a Spirit-directed application of *all* the principles revealed therein. Perhaps the most instructive passages in connection with the question of this chapter are those which relate His teachings concerning Samaritans. And of those passages (see Lk 9: 52; 17:16; Jn 4:9, 39), undoubtedly the story of the good Samaritan (Lk 10:30-37) is the capstone. The story was given in answer to the question "Who is my neighbor?" (10:29). The answer is, then, the person who is in need, and particularly that one whose path crosses mine, regardless of economic, political, national, or racial differences.

That phrase *whose path crosses mine* is very important. It is very easy to talk about concern for the needy or the poor without having concern for any particular needy or poor person. This is not to say that the believer has no responsibility to those whom he has never seen, but it is to say that concern for a group can only be genuinely demonstrated by doing something for one or more in that group.

Involvement. The Christian should be an involved person. Top priority should be given to giving the gospel to all people, for this is our Lord's command. Doing good to all men, especially to fellow believers, is also commanded (Gal 6:10). No individual or nation is condemned for being wealthy by comparison with others. It is how the wealth is acquired and the uses to which it is put that concern God. Standing and working within the law against illegalities and injustices is a Christian duty; being a political revolutionary is forbidden (1 Pe 2:13-15). Every command which relates believers to other believers is to be obeyed without racial prejudice. This certainly includes receiving into a local church all believers who present themselves to that church.

The path of obedience to these commands as they work out in various practical situations is not always as clear as the commands. Many of the practical problems which Christians face involve more sociological than theological factors. The believer will not find specific answers in the Bible to every problem and situation he may face, and he cannot help but be influenced by sociological factors. For example, we recognize that the New Testament does not forbid interracial marriage; neither does it command it.* Yet the factors involved in raising children of such a marriage may influence the decision to contract the marriage. And those factors are different in Hawaii, for instance, from what they are in some southern state.

The Bible does not condemn a man's preferring to belong to one sound church instead of a different but equally sound one. But it severely condemns partiality in any group, whatever be the manifestation of it. Class prejudice is just as wrong as racial prejudice. Some New Testament churches may have had slaves as elders ruling over their own masters whom they served otherwise.

The question of the gospel and society is tangent to but really beyond the scope of this chapter. Suffice it to say that the principal message of the New Testament is centered in the death of Christ for our salvation. When the

*Timothy was born into a home of mixed parentage, his father being a Gentile and his mother a Jew (Ac 16:1). While anthropologists generally do not use the word *race* to refer to Jews or Gentiles, *Webster's Third New International Dictionary* defines *race* as "a class or kind of individuals with common characteristics, interests, appearances, or habits as if derived from a common ancestor" and gives the Jewish race as an example.

message is stated (as in 1 Co 15:3-5) it is not stated in terms of the social, cultural, and other human benefits of the truth. We must never put the cart before the horse in our Christian witness. A. N. Triton has given a fine summary of the matter:

> The Bible is concerned for society, but there is no such thing as a social gospel. There is social law. There is also a gospel of salvation in Christ which has far-reaching repercussions in society when men who have entered into the experience of the gospel go to live it out. True Christians will seek to grow increasingly like Christ. We must follow Him "who went about doing good", or we are bogus Christians. History amply bears this out. The great periods of social impact have followed and not preceded the periods of revival of personal faith. No sooner has the attention of the church been diverted from our relationship to God than the effectiveness of the church in society has begun steadily to decline. By and large it is people who were in the New Testament sense other-worldly-minded who have had the most effect on this world. Those who have been shown the supreme greatness and unique merit of Christ and His cross should be those who are the most concerned to live in love, in accordance with His commands, and to see that God should rule over all men and that His Word should be obeyed in all spheres.[1]

6

The Question of Situation Ethics

"Thou shalt not commit adultery—ordinarily."

"Thou shalt not steal—usually."

"Thou shalt not covet—generally."

This is the way some say Joseph Fletcher rewrote the commandments with his *Situation Ethics*. Shake loose infantile dependence on laws and systems of morality, decide moral issues situationally, and learn to "sin bravely," he declared, so that we can live as free men. Agape love is the key to right action even though that action per se is sinful. "Lying could be more Christian than telling the truth. Stealing could be better than respecting private property. No action is good or right in itself. It depends on whether it hurts or helps people, whether or not it serves love's purpose—understanding love to be personal concern—*in the situation*."[1]

Many responded to the new ethic with great enthusiasm, but there were also many critics. Harvey Cox attributed Fletcher's acceptance to "the simple fact that Americans as a whole are better educated and they reflect this added sophistication in their ethical and religious attitudes."[2] But an editorial in the secular press criticized Fletcher and his teaching in no uncertain terms. It said in part:

We must suppose that as a replacement for old-fashioned followers of Christ, these modernists would convert us all to mini-Christians. . . . What it is, is a deterioration in morals. . . . Fletcher goes on with his wool gathering. . . . Unfortunately, Dr. Fletcher's sophistry attracts many young people. It is always tempting to take the easy way out. . . . We can always expect a rush of followers, who try to rationalize their own moral deterioration by saying what they are doing is in reality a "modern" approach to religion.

The dictionary has an apt definition for the sophism employed by Dr. Fletcher: "Sophism—an argument used for deception, disputation, or the display of intellectual brilliance; an argument that is correct in form or appearance but is actually invalid."

That's Dr. Fletcher and his "situation ethics."[3]

THE TEACHINGS OF SITUATION ETHICS

Just who is this man Fletcher and what is it that he believes, not as interpreted by his friends or foes, but as articulated in his own writings? Joseph Fletcher (b. 1905) has worked as a coal miner, a laborer in a rope factory, a social worker, and a college chaplain. For twenty-seven years he was professor of social ethics at the Episcopal Theological School in Cambridge, Massachusetts, later teaching ethics at the University of Virginia Medical School. Cox calls him a "spokesman for social Christianity grounded in essential piety."[4]

Fletcher's book *Situation Ethics: The New Morality* appeared first in 1966. It was followed the next year by a book called *Moral Responsibility* which is a compilation of miscellaneous addresses and articles done at various times. In the former book his position is clearly stated, and this is it in a capsule.

First he discusses three approaches to ethics. At one extreme is the approach of legalism, which he identifies as any system that gets its authority from a rule book, like the Bible. At the opposite extreme is antinomianism which has no rules, like libertinism, Moral Rearmament Movement, and existentialism. But right in the middle (and thus presumably the best by its balanced position!) is situationalism. It is not, he insists, existential, because it uses our heritage, moral judgment, and love as guidelines.

Second, he states some presuppositions of his position, using philosophical terms. He says that situation ethics involves pragmatism (because it lets the present situation guide); relativism (because, according to Fletcher, one must never say never or always or perfect or absolute); positivism (because at its heart is the positive declaration, which cannot be proved, that love is the key category for conduct); and personalism (because people, not things, are of primary importance).

Third (and this is the heart of his creed), he states the propositions which serve as principles to guide situational ethical conduct. They are these.

1. Love is the only thing that is intrinsically good. This is agape love, and it is the only good thing that is.

2. The ruling norm for Christian decision is love.

3. Love and justice are the same, because justice is love using its head.

4. Love is not necessarily liking, for love wills the neighbor's good whether we like him or not. Thus love is impartial.

5. Only the end justifies the means; nothing else. Of course, the end is love, but he argues that a loving end

justifies any means, including lies, adultery, stealing, murder. However, Fletcher says that we need to ask four questions about any action in order to "hallow" the means used. They are: What is the end desired? What are the means that will achieve that end? What is the motive for using those means (it should be responsible love)? And, what are the foreseeable consequences? Answering these questions will place some governors on the means used.

6. These five propositions give content to a sixth by telling what a good end is, so that love decides then and there in the situation. Love is not prescriptive but situational. However, it seems that the very existence of the first five propositions (with the four questions under the fifth) contradicts the sixth. Has not Fletcher given precepts to be followed in any situation before the situation arises? And if he has, then how can he say that love decides *then and there*, since it is not prescriptive but situational? The sixth proposition makes the first five unnecessary, or the first five make the sixth impossible. Of course, Fletcher would say that even these rules are of no intrinsic value, but rather they are guidelines to guard our behavior so that it will be helpful in any particular situation.

The case for the new morality is illustrated almost convincingly. Perhaps the best-known illustration which Fletcher uses is Mrs. Bergmeier. She was a German captured by the Russians and taken off to a prison camp in the Ukraine. Her husband, who had been previously captured by the Allies and who spent time in a POW camp in Wales, was eventually returned to his home in Berlin. After much searching, he located and was reunited with his three children, but the whereabouts of the mother remained a mystery. Meanwhile, Mrs. Bergmeier learned that her family was together and searching for her, but the only way she could leave the camp was either for medical reasons (which would only mean transfer to a Soviet hospital) or pregnancy (in which case she would be returned to Germany). She thought about her situation and finally asked a friendly guard to impregnate her, which he did. So she was returned to her family who welcomed her with open arms even after she told them how she managed to gain her freedom. Indeed, as the story goes, the family loved baby Dietrich more than all the rest since he had done more for them than anybody. Fletcher calls Mrs. Bergmeier's act "sacrificial adultery," for she loved her family so much (the motive) that she was willing to commit adultery (the means, not sinful in this case) to be reunited with them (the end, desirable in this case).

Or there is the story of the Christian girl who was asked by American intelligence to prostitute herself in the interests of gaining information from the enemy. The basis on which she was approached was this: if your brother who fought in the last war risked his life for his country, why cannot you give at least your body for your country?[5]

These are thought-provoking situations, and they ask loudly, Do the rules really apply to our modern society? Is not a situation ethic really more loving and just?

SOME PROBLEMS OF SITUATION ETHICS

A basic problem with situation ethics is that it does not give proper place to a living God who has spoken and who acts in history concerning the affairs of men. This is not to say that those who hold these views do not have any kind

of God in their system, but it is to insist that they have dis-
carded the true God who has revealed Himself in the Bible
and in historical time-space activities. Indeed, the God of
the situationist is not the supernatural, transcendent Being
revealed in the Scriptures. While Fletcher states the new
morality from the popular ethical side, Bishop John A. T.
Robinson expounds it on the popular theological front
(having been influenced in his thinking by Paul Tillich).
On the connection between one's concept of God and one's
ethics, Robinson said: "And it is impossible to reassess one's
doctrine of God, of how one understands the transcendent,
without bringing one's view of morality into the same melt-
ing-pot."[6] And what is his concept of God? He said, "But
the god it [naturalism] is bowing out is the God of the 'su-
pernaturalist' way of thinking."[7] In other words, when one
changes (and thus rejects) the God of the Bible, then one's
ethics change too. This permits Mrs. Bergmeier's family
and friends to say that she had done a good and right thing.

Situationists do not fully accept the fact that this real
God may have spoken and that what He said is to be regarded as truth to be obeyed. Actually, they do not completely reject this idea, for they want to hold onto some
echoes of the biblical revelation. Fletcher states that situation ethics "goes part of the way with scriptural law by
accepting revelation as the source of the norm while rejecting all 'revealed' norms or laws but the one command—
to love God in the neighbor."[8] He wants to eat his cake
and have it too!

Notice, however, that when the Lord gave the two greatest commandments, He gave them as coordinate statements
("Thou shalt love the Lord . . . Thou shalt love thy neighbor.") The situationist has made them read: "Thou shalt

love the Lord thy God *by* loving thy neighbor." In this way he cleverly takes the attention away from the first (which the Lord said was the greatest of all commandments), if not actually obliterates it. And this is the heart of the problem with situation ethics—there is no vertical dimension in it! Ethics is totally related to the horizontal—to the neighbor, to the situation, to circumstances. When God is no longer supernatural, He can be eliminated. Such a God has not spoken, so His laws can be ignored. And such a God does not intervene in man's life, so the choices facing one in a particular situation never need include the possibility of the miraculous. Neither do they need to include the concept of sacrifice in the will of God. Thus Mr. and Mrs. Bergmeier did not have to consider either the option that a living God could open the prison doors in some way other than by sinning, or the option that separation or even martyrdom might be to the glory of God. This is the basic fallacy of situation ethics—God is not supernatural; His Word is meaningless; His interacting in lives today is impossible.

A second problem concerns agape love, which is the key to the new morality; but it is a key which will not unlock the doors of solutions to ethical problems. For situationalists define their agape love as "loving the unlovable."[9] The Bible defines it as that quality of God Himself which is given to man only through the supernatural work of the Holy Spirit (Ro 5:5). Since situation ethics' agape is human, it will inevitably be tinged with hypocrisy and dishonesty. These are built-in factors in any human agape. Bishop Pike saw this clearly: "This would mean that hypocrisy is built in—is part of the very nature of agape. To tell the truth presents a different problem from making an existential decision, where all the factors are weighed in a given context. . . . Dishonesty is inherent in full agape."[10]

Pike unfortunately did not offer a solution to the deficiency he saw, but the Bible does. The fruit of the Spirit is love, but no unregenerate person can bear such fruit, and, of course, the necessity to be born again is not part of the theology of the new morality. Thus the very key needed is not attainable because of rejection of the Person who alone can give it.

The Biblical Teaching

The Bible, of course, has a great deal to say about ethical conduct, and the biblical teaching is totally different from that of situation ethics.

For one thing, the biblical view includes specific laws. If God, for example, has prohibited adultery (Ex 20:14), and if there has been no abrogation of that commandment (Ro 13:9), then committing adultery is a violation of God's expressed law and is therefore sin. Indeed, specifics of Old Testament law are often heightened in the New Testament. For instance, not only is stealing forbidden by the Decalogue and the New Testament, but in the New Testament the believer is enjoined to work in order to have money and things to give to those in need (Eph 4:28). And it goes without saying that these biblical laws are authoritative.

For another thing, the Bible gives guidelines for those situations and circumstances to which specific laws do not speak. There are several such guidelines:

1. In debatable situations the believer is never to use his liberty in a manner which will hinder the spiritual progress of another believer (1 Co 8). This guideline

concerns action and activities which have moral value only extrinsically, not intrinsically. The moral value is determined by the effect of the action on others. In the text referred to, the matter was that of whether or not a believer was at liberty to eat meats that had been sacrificed to idols when they were slaughtered. Some felt they could not eat such meat; others felt they could. Actually Paul says that since the sacrificing to the idol was an invalid transaction, eating would really make no difference. But not all realized that, and some still ate as if under the spell of the idol. Therefore, Paul concludes, for their sakes one's liberty should be restricted. This is how agape love serves others (Gal 5: 13).

2. Another principle is that of acting in all situations so as to promote the glory of God (1 Co 10:31). The glory of God is the display of God and thus means conformity to what He has revealed of Himself in His Word. Thus the application of this principle in a situation really involves prior knowledge of what God is like and therefore what He would desire in any situation, which knowledge can be acquired with certainty only from the Bible.

3. Another principle is expressed in Colossians 4:5: "Walk in wisdom toward them that are without, redeeming the time." The purpose of wise actions is to win those outside of Christ to Him. What particular course of action this may require in each instance, God will reveal to the individual believer. This principle does not need to be used if one does not believe that people are lost and need to be won to Christ.

While we acknowledge that there may be differences of opinion as to the specific application of these guidelines, the guidelines themselves are clear and set the bounds of our actions. One might summarize by saying that the biblical teaching includes law plus agape.

Finally, it should be reiterated that the love which is imperative in the application of the biblical guidelines and laws is the true agape from God. It is not the situationist's agape of his wishful thinking, but the real dynamic of the regenerated life through the power of the indwelling Holy Spirit. This is the motivation to want to keep the commandments of God's revealed will. This is the motivation for being willing to limit one's liberty for the sake of a brother. It is the dimension for proper conduct which only God can supply and only to believers. Without it, situation ethics is a dangerous existentialism; with it, God guides and acts in the situation through the believer in complete accord with His character and will to the praise of His glory.

7

The Question of Suicide

DEATH BY SUICIDE claims the lives of more than twenty thousand people every year in the United States alone. Our awareness of its frequency is probably not so acute as it could be simply because the obituary often reads, "She died at home," or "He died while on a business trip." But hushing up the means cannot obscure the fact that thousands of people—believers and unbelievers alike—are taking their own lives. The Bible has some sobering things to say that are extremely pertinent to the matter of suicide.

SUICIDE BREAKS THE COMMANDMENT OF GOD

The sanctity of human life is paramount in the sixth commandment, "Thou shalt not kill" (Ex 20:13). Here murder is condemned, and elsewhere in the law every act that endangers human life is condemned, whether the act arise from carelessness (Deu 22:8), wantonness (Lev 19: 14), hatred, anger, or revenge (Lev 19:17-18). Human life is sacred, for man was made in the image of God (Gen 9:6, where also this same sanctity is made the basis for capital punishment). But the commandment has no direct object. It does not say, "Thou shalt not kill someone" or "Thou shalt not kill thy fellowman." It is simply, "Thou

shalt not kill." Thus it has to be concluded that "the prohibition includes not only the killing of a fellow-man, but
the destruction of one's own life, or suicide."[1] This conclusion should not be surprising, for if God does consider
human life so sacred, one cannot say that means all human
life except his own, which he then has a right to end at his
choice of time and circumstances. Suicide negates God's
estimate of life and violates the sixth commandment (Ro
13:9).

SUICIDE DOES NOT END IT ALL

Often those who commit suicide leave notes indicating,
among other things, why they chose that course of action.
Frequently, the reason involves the desire to end it all.
For various reasons life became empty or its circumstances
too difficult to bear, and they felt that death would bring
release from all their problems.

Our Lord made it quite clear that a person continues
conscious existence after the death of the body. Indeed,
it is only the body that dies, and the immaterial part of
the person not only continues to exist but apparently can
remember (Lk 16:25). Suicide, then, cannot even kill the
memories of the things which may have driven the individual to suicide.

Passages which speak of judgment which will come to all
men also show that death does not end it all. "It is ap-
pointed unto men once to die, but after this the judgment"
(Heb 9:27). The scene at the great white throne where
the unsaved of all ages will be judged is an awesome one.
The dead are raised to stand before the throne, and they
are to be judged according to the works done in their
mortal bodies (Rev 20:12-13). Not only does death not

end it all, but the activities of life (including suicide) will be reviewed after death. This ought to be a deterrent to anyone contemplating suicide.

CAN A BELIEVER COMMIT SUICIDE?

Of course he can, for obviously believers do. But, some may say, are you sure such are genuine believers? Some Christians are quite sure that a true believer cannot commit suicide, but there is no scriptural evidence for such a claim. Others, who maintain that a believer may lose his salvation, feel that if a Christian takes his own life, then he loses his salvation and is destined to the lake of fire. That true believers cannot commit suicide seems open to serious question, since many apparently do. Though experience is not always a safe guide, it would be very difficult to judge certain well-known and widely used men of God as unbelievers because they did commit suicide. Is there any biblical example of a believer who committed suicide? Actually there is none in the New Testament (Judas was not a believer), but in the Old Testament there is the suicide of King Saul who fell on his own sword. Whether or not Saul was a believer is debated. Some take the statement of Samuel (1 Sa 28:19) that soon Saul and his sons would be with him to mean that Saul would be in paradise or heaven with Samuel. Others understand this to mean merely that Saul would soon die and go to Sheol, which included the place of the wicked dead as well. So the statement is ambiguous, and we cannot prove conclusively that Saul was a believer who committed suicide.

Nevertheless we do know that believers do not lose their salvation beause of certain kinds of sin. Admittedly suicide is a sin (for it is murder of self), but adultery and murder of someone else are also equally gross sins. Yet we know that King David, who committed both of those sins, did not lose his salvation because of it (Ro 4:7-8). The blood of Jesus Christ cleanses from all sin, including suicide.

THE EFFECTS OF SUICIDE

We have already noted that suicide doesn't end it all for the individual. For others who are left, the effect is always one of sorrow and often of increased complications. If a family is left, it is deprived of the presence and help of the one who takes his own life. A believer who ends his life also ends forever his opportunities to witness and serve the Lord on earth. In a sense suicide is one of the greatest acts of selfishness, for in it the individual caters to his desires and own will and ignores the effects it has on others.

People on the brink of suicide often suffer from an overpowering sense of being alone. The accompanying depression shrinks the horizons of the individual until his entire perspective is filled only with himself. This leads to self-pity and to the self-deception that justifies in his mind the final act of suicide. Self-centeredness is a root of suicide.

But, it is argued, if that one is bedfast or so neurotic as to be useless, then there is no selfishness involved in taking his own life. But by what standard are you measuring usefulness? When I first began to teach, one of the people who prayed for me the most frequently and fervently was a lady who could only get out of bed if her husband lifted her into a wheelchair. The hours, days, months, and years of her confinement were filled with the most useful kind of service on behalf of people all over this world. Sometimes God uses even the total incapacity of someone in the lives of the family that is obliged to care for him. Also, neuroses and psychoses are not always permanent. Cures are discovered, and God still heals. But suicide gives no opportunity for a cure or for a demonstration of the power of God.

Since a believer does not lose his salvation when he commits suicide, is he not with Christ which is far better (Phil 1:23)? To be in heaven would seem to be more desirable than to be on earth in an intolerable situation. Before embracing that conclusion, look at the logical ramification of it. If that logic is true, then all believers ought to commit suicide, for being in heaven would be better. It is true that to depart and be with Christ is far better *if* the departure is according to God's perfect timing. If the departure is out of the will of God, then the result is not far better. When death occurs, by whatever means, the believer's life of service here is finished, and it is that service which will be examined at the judgment seat of Christ. The outcome of the judgment does not involve the eternal destiny of the believer, for that is not in question. The matter in question is reward or loss of it. And it is that phrase "he shall suffer loss" (1 Co 3:15) which is one of the significant effects of the suicide of a believer. The word *loss* means to forfeit, or in the passive, as here, to suffer forfeit of what one possessed or might have possessed. John warns of the same possibility of losing a full reward (2 Jn 8). Since suicide does break the command of God, then the one who commits it must suffer loss at the judgment seat of Christ. The compassion we have for anyone caught in any sin must not obscure what the Bible teaches about the consequences of that sin.

THE DEFENSES AGAINST SUICIDE

No Christian need commit suicide, but the flesh is weak, Satan is powerful, and circumstances often adverse. What are his defenses against this sin?

On the negative side, he should remember that the specific command of God forbids it; that it inevitably brings sorrow to those who are left; that it gives vent to his selfish concerns rather than doing the will of God; that it will be reviewed, along with his other deeds, at the judgment seat of Christ (2 Co 5:10) ; and that it is in the final analysis an act of rebellion against God. These are sobering facts which, properly considered, should be powerful deterrents to anyone contemplating suicide.

On the positive side, the Christian remembers that he is heir to all the promises of God. If he feels driven to the point of suicide because of getting out of the will of God, then he should use God's remedies for restoring fellowship. Confession of sins to God is first, then righting wronged relationships must follow. This will sometimes involve much time and patience. But renewed fellowship with the Father will remove the desire to escape the consequences of sin through suicide. If he is driven through adverse circumstances which are not the result of sin, then he must try to understand that he is in the particular situation in the will of God. Even though the Lord may use Satan to bring about the combination of circumstances, to endure triumphantly is the will of God. Job is, of course, the best example of such. Sometimes God will deliver, and sometimes He will not, but in either case He promises a way to escape "that ye may be able to bear it" (1 Co 10:13) . Bearing does not necessarily mean relief. Notice that the miraculous deliverances recorded in Hebrews 11:32-35 are followed immediately by the record of many who were not delivered (vv. 36-37). The promise of 1 Corinthians 10: 13 guarantees that God will limit the intensity and kind of test to what He knows we can individually bear. And His knowledge is without limit, so the promise is not based on what we think we can bear, but on what He knows we can. No believer has the right to say that God expected too much of him in the light of this promise. Even when the apostle Paul despaired of life itself, God was carefully controlling the measure of his tests (2 Co 1:8-10; 6:4-10). God's servants have sometimes been so severely tested that they wished for death (1 Ki 19:4; Jn 4:8), but they did not take the matter into their own hands, and God rescued them.

But are there not instances when people, overwhelmed by pressures or depressions, take their own lives in a state of temporary insanity? Undoubtedly there are, but it is difficult to know to what extent such people are responsible for actions done when they are not themselves. There are degrees of irrationality; and while the climactic act of suicide may apparently be uncontrollable, the steps that lead to it are usually not. It is clear that an unsaved person who commits suicide ends all further opportunity to be saved, whether that suicide is done in a sane or insane condition. Though all the sins of a believer are forgiven, the believer who commits suicide, whether sane or not, loses further opportunities of service in this life. We must leave the judging of such cases to God who knows perfectly all the circumstances involved.

8

The Question of Abortion

WITH THE LIBERALIZING of the laws regarding abortion and the sweeping decision of the Supreme Court of January 22, 1973, which overthrew the abortion statutes of the State of Texas, there have followed widespread discussion and debate within many groups concerning this question. The American Baptist Convention, the Episcopal Church, the United Methodist Church, the United Presbyterian Church, and the Lutheran Church in America have adopted formal resolutions favoring repeal of laws against abortion and placing the responsibility for the decision in the hands of the woman or couple involved. Christian publications have carried articles on the subject by theologians, ministers, physicians, and professors of ethics.

Much of what has been written discusses situations and circumstances involved in decisions regarding possible abortion without reference to the Bible at all. While it is true that the Bible does not say a great deal about this subject, there are biblical truths which throw light on the matter and which, therefore, must be considered by the Christian.

THE DEFINITION OF ABORTION

Abortion is the expulsion of the human fetus prematurely (that is, before it is capable of surviving outside the womb). Accident may cause an abortion, or artificial means may induce one. A therapeutic abortion is done when the termination of the pregnancy is necessary for the sake of the mother's physical health; a psychiatric abortion, for her mental health. Eugenic abortion is used as a means of keeping retarded or deformed children from being born; social abortion is used to ease economic pressure on a family; ethical abortion is used in cases of rape or incest; and abortion-on-demand permits abortion for any or no reason. Since there is no control over spontaneous abortion (which some say happens to about 30 percent of all fertilized eggs), this kind of abortion is eliminated from this discussion. We are concerned with induced abortion, particularly abortion on demand.

Scriptural Evidence

Undoubtedly one of the principal reasons for the many different opinions concerning abortion among those who hold to the authority of the Scriptures is that there are so few direct statements bearing on the subject. However, there are some germane passages which must be considered.

Exodus 21:22-24. "And if men strive together, and hurt a woman with child, so that her fruit depart, and yet no harm follow; he shall . . . pay as the judges determine. But if any harm follow, then thou shalt give life for life, eye for eye, tooth for tooth" (ASV). A more literal translation of verse 22 is this: "And when men struggle with each other and strike a pregnant women so that her children come out, yet there is not harm, he shall surely be fined as the woman's husband lays on him; and he [the husband] shall set [the fine] with arbitrators."

There are two principal interpretations of "so that her fruit depart." One understands it to mean a premature birth of the child, and the fine is assessed because the life of the child might have been harmed. Of course, if the child that is prematurely born does not live, then the *lex talionis* (the principle of an eye for an eye and a life for a life from Lev 24:17-20) applied.[1] The other interpretation considers this as referring to the accidental miscarriage of the fetus, and the fine is imposed as an indemnification to the father because the fetus was lost. If the mother also should die in the accident, then the *lex talionis* applied.[2]

This second viewpoint sees a major difference in the penalty imposed for the death of the fetus (a fine) and the penalty imposed in case of the death of the mother (the death of the one who caused the accident). This difference is understood to indicate that the fetus is not considered a "soul," no matter how far gestation has progressed. If this line of reasoning is taken one step farther, then it may lend support to the conclusion that induced abortion is permitted. The logic is this: since the penalties are quite different, the fetus is not a "soul"; and since the fetus is not a soul, its induced expulsion is permitted even today.

Of course, it is quite a jump from the law of Exodus 21: 22-25 which concerns accidental abortion to the contemporary question of induced abortion; nevertheless, this viewpoint says that since the former was only fined, the latter is permitted. Actually the only point in the passage which relates to the subject of induced abortion is the statement that accidental abortion does not make the one who caused it a murderer and therefore under the penalty of breaking the sixth commandment. However, since the passage only considers the case of accidental abortion, to say that it allows for or at least does not forbid induced abortion is to make a logical leap that is not supported by the text.

One must also consider the possibility that the interpretation that the passage refers to accidental miscarriage may not be the correct one. The first interpretation (that it refers to a live, though premature, birth) in reality has better support. The verb translated "depart" or "come out" (*yatsa*) usually refers in the Old Testament to a live birth (see Gen 25:25-26; 35:11; 38:28-30; Ex 1:5; Deu 28:57; 2 Sa 16:11; 1 Ch 1:12; Job 1:21; 3:11; Ec 5:15; Jer 20:18). In no case is the word used to indicate a miscarriage. (Its use in Numbers 12:12 refers to the birth of a stillborn child.) The usual verb for miscarriage (*shakol*) is found in Exodus 23:26 and Hosea 9:14. Thus the Hebrew word used in Exodus 21:22 indicates a premature birth, not miscarriage, and does not concern abortion at all.

To sum up: by the interpretation that sees Exodus 21:22-25 referring to accidental miscarriage, it may be concluded that since only a fine is levied, there is a difference between the kind of life of an unborn child and that of an adult, and further that the one who caused the accident is not a murderer. By the interpretation that understands the passage to refer to premature birth, it must be concluded that God values viable fetuses the same as He does adults, since the *lex talionis* applies if the child is born dead. Neither interpretation, of course, speaks directly to the question of induced abortion or lends support for the practice of induced abortion.

Psalm 139:13. "For thou didst form my inward parts [veins]: Thou didst cover [knit] me together in my mother's womb" (ASV). In this verse the protection and possession of God over the unborn are clearly stated. God's concern and creative power are extended to prenatal life. This teaching would make it impossible to consider the embryo or fetus "just a piece of tissue" or "an insensible blob of tissue." The very least one must say is that at the moment of conception there exists a potential human being (or better, a human being with potential) which is sacred and valuable to God, as evidenced by God's personal involvement. To be sure, the fetus develops and enters a different stage of life at birth, but there does seem to be a continuous line of life from conception until death. Even if life in the womb is not the same as it is after birth, it is human life in a certain form. And it is life which God is intimately concerned about.

This concept is borne out by God's relationship to certain people who were yet unborn. Of Jeremiah it is said: "Before I formed thee in the belly [womb] I knew thee; and before thou camest forth out of the womb I sanctified thee, and I ordained thee a prophet unto the nations" (Jer 1:5). Of Jacob and Esau in their mother's womb God said, "Two nations are in thy womb, and two manner of people shall be separated from thy bowels [born of thee]; and the one people shall be stronger than the other people; and the elder shall serve the younger" (Gen 25:23).

In Psalm 51:5, David confesses that he was conceived in sin. "The iniquity and sin meant are not those of his mother, but his own."[3] This important passage establishes the humanness of the fetus since guilt is attached to it and since only humans and angels can be guilty of sin. The act of conceiving is not sin, but man from his conception onward is tainted with sin and is guilty before God. This can only be true if humanness is ascribed to the fetus.

Though the biblical teaching is scanty, we can conclude that the unborn child is not nonhuman, but is a life that is of concern to God; that miscarriage due to an accident is not murder; and that induced abortion takes life which is related to God, known by Him, and guilty before Him.

THEOLOGICAL CONSIDERATIONS

However one views the fetus and the matter of ensoulment, there can be no debate that the destruction of it destroys the life that would have developed from it and thus the person that would have taken his or her place in the world. Obviously, everything that develops from the fetus is destroyed if the fetus is destroyed.

This raises certain theological considerations which need to be thought about in connection with induced abortion. One concerns the matter of the glory of God. We do know that a physical deformity with which a person is born can be for the glory of God. The blind man of John 9 was born that way, and although the disciples, following a common belief of the times, thought that this was a punishment for sin, the Lord clearly stated that it was so "the works of God should be made manifest in him" (Jn 9:3).

Now try to think of the implications of the following line of reasoning (hypothetical though it be!). Suppose a prenatal test could have shown that this baby boy was to be born without sight. The parents might have been advised to consider sparing themselves the problems of rearing such a child by terminating the pregnancy. Suppose abortion was easily and legally available in Palestine. Should they abort the fetus or not? Imagine, further, that they did decide to have the abortion. Obviously the baby would not have been born, the child would not have grown up, and he would not have been the means of demonstrating the works of God. Undoubtedly there would have been some other blind person on whom the Lord could have performed the miracle, but that man and his family would have missed the experience.

The point is simply this: a defective child may be the direct gift of God to a family as an instrument for the greater glory of God. An amazing present-day illustration of this is related in the book *Melissa Comes Home.*[4] A retarded child born into the Krentel home became the means of leading her parents to establish a home for such children, involving many miracles from the Lord and blessing to many families. And as the story has become more widely known, God has been more widely glorified, all because of the gift of a retarded child to a believing family.

A second consideration concerns the principle of Romans 8:28: for the believer "all things work together for good." Chrysostom said: "When he says 'all things,' he means even things that seem to be painful. For even if affliction, poverty, imprisonment, hunger, death, or any other thing should come upon thee, God is able to turn all these the contrary way. Since this also is part of His ineffable power, to make what things seem troublesome light to us, and turn them to our help."[5] Thus the "unwanted child" may bring greater good into the life of a family in fulfillment of this promise.

Is there, then, any justification for abortion? It would appear that one might justifiably abort a fetus if at any stage there is material aggression against the mother. Such abortion would be in the nature of self-defense. Psychiatric abortion is, in my judgment, a different matter. Another has well summarized the objections. "Psychiatric reasons are among the most common reasons given as the grounds for abortion. But this is very flexible ground; it can be used easily to justify abortion in all kinds of circumstances. One writer summarizes: 'Frankly, in psychiatry the question of abortion is more often raised because the pregnancy is unwanted than because of clear and serious risk to the mental health of the mother.' . . . I would only add that in some cases the cure might be worse than the illness, because it could put a heavy burden of guilt on the soul of the mother concerned."[6]

Other reasons for abortion, such as preventing the over-burdening of a family with a deformed child, or easing the economic strain, do not have scriptural warrant. The following declaration of some of the best minds in Christendom today seems much too open-ended: "The Christian physician will advise induced abortion only to safeguard greater values sanctioned by Scripture. These values should include individual health, family welfare, and social responsibility."[7] While there are such values and they are valid ones, so also are the glory of God and the will of God, which are actually more weighty considerations.

Finally, there is a very important ramification of this entire discussion. Dr. Carl F. H. Henry put it well when he wrote:

> A Christian response to the abortion-crisis encourages a new respect and sense of responsibility for the body and its use. A woman's body is not the domain and property of others. It is hers to control, and she alone is responsible to God and to society, for its use. When she yields that control, and through pregnancy is involved in intraper-

sonal relationships with a second party, and through conception to a third party, and indeed to human society as a
whole, it becomes too late for her to justify abortion on
the basis of self-determination. The God of creation and
redemption is also the guardian of the womb, however
much abortion-on-demand would contradict or scorn such
a conviction.[8]

9

The Question of Demon Activity

WHEN I FIRST BEGAN to teach, it was necessary to spend much more time trying to establish the existence of Satan and demons than it is today. Churches of Satan, Ouija boards, tarot cards, and even bumper stickers proclaiming the drivers are warlocks or witches all bombard us with evidence of what seems to be satanic and demonic activity. Today, most people recognize that Satan and demons do exist and are at work in the world.

THE ORIGIN AND CHARACTERISTICS OF DEMONS

The origin of demons has been a matter of speculation for centuries. The Greeks said that they were the souls of departed evil people. Some Christians believe that they are the disembodied spirits of a race of people who lived and died before Adam was created. However, the Scriptures say nothing about such a race. More likely, demons are the angels who revolted with Satan. Notice their close link with him in Matthew 12:24 and 25:41. Too, they are called spirit beings (albeit unclean; Mt 17:18, cf. Mk 9:25) which associates them with the spirit world rather than the human.

Though they are spirit beings, they are not omnipresent. Each demon can be in only one place at any given moment. The very fact that they can be confined demonstrates their lack of omnipresence (Mk 5:13; 2 Pe 2:4). Neither are they omniscient, though they do possess a high degree of intelligence. Their long existence and great experience with people under almost every conceivable circumstance adds to their intelligence.

The Activities of Demons

The activities of demons mentioned in many passages in the Bible can be cataloged into three categories: they promote a system of doctrine; they seek to destroy men's bodies and souls; and they deceive men and nations.

They promote a system of doctrine. "But the Spirit saith expressly, that in later times some shall fall away from the faith, giving heed to seducing spirits and doctrines of demons, through the hypocrisy of men that speak lies, branded in their own conscience as with a hot iron; forbidding to marry, and commanding to abstain from meats, which God created to be received with thanksgiving by them them that believe and know the truth" (1 Ti 4:1-3, ASV).

The expression "in later times" refers "to a period future to the speaker. . . . In the apostasy of the present the inspired Apostle sees the commencement of the fuller apostasy of the future."[1] Thus demonic doctrine has been increasing and will continue to increase in the church, reaching a climax at the end of the age.

That this false system of teaching originates from demons is clear, but the text also says that it is promoted through men who speak the lies. Comparing this passage with 1 John 2:19 and 4:3, it appears that demonic spirits directly empower human anti-Christian teachers and supply them with source material for their teaching. This close association between Satan, demons, and human beings is seen also in 2 Corinthians 11:13-15 . Notice, too, that deception is the hallmark of Satan's procedure for disseminating false doctrine. One would expect, therefore, to find this aspect of demonic activity centering in churches and radiating from pulpits rather than from, say, mental institutions.

What is included in the doctrine of demons? There seem to be two principal emphases. First, they promote a works salvation (1 Ti 4:3-4). This effort to promote salvation by works will emphasize asceticism in the lives of those who accept it. Abstaining from marriage and from eating meat will apparently make the devotees feel that they are commending themselves to God and therefore that they have no need of a Saviour from sin. It is interesting to observe today that abstention from meat is coming into certain Christian youth circles as a carry-over from teaching of eastern religions. Of course, demons do not always promote asceticism; often they are actively engaged in promoting evil in the lives of men. Victor Ernest said:

> The spirits I encountered at seances were for the most part very moralistic. . . . In contrast to the high moral and ethical tone of the seances in other homes, I attended some where the spirits were blasphemous and sensual. . . . Even the spirits who told us to improve ourselves morally and spiritually were doing so to gain our allegiance for themselves and keep us from God himself.[2]

But encouraging asceticism has a more obvious purpose in seeking to establish a works basis for salvation, for man has little or no sense of need when he thinks he is living a good life.

Second, demonic doctrine will seek to make the Saviour Jesus Christ worthless by denying the fact that He is the God-man. This can be done by denying either the deity of Christ or His humanity.

A denial of the deity of Christ occurred in the apostle John's day (1 Jn 2:22-23) in the form of denying the Son's equal position in the Trinity. Commenting on this, another has said:

> A common "Gnostic" theory was that "the aeon Christ" descended upon the man Jesus at His baptism, and left Him before the Passion. Those who held such a doctrine denied that "Jesus was the Christ"; and in so denying, denied the union of the divine and human in one Person. . . . The denial of the personal union of true manhood and true Godhead in Christ involves the denial of the essential relations of Fatherhood and Sonship in the Divine Nature.[3]

A denial of the humanity of Christ was also prevalent in John's day (1 Jn 4:2-3). This involved denying the mode of His coming (in the flesh) and the permanence of the incarnation (since the tense of "come" is perfect). If the Lord Jesus was not both God and man, He was not a sufficient Saviour, and this is why demons attack either or both aspects of the true doctrine of the God-man. The Saviour had to be a human being in order to be able to die, for God cannot die; and He had to be God in order for that death to be an effective payment for sins. To deny His humanity makes it impossible for Him to die; to deny His deity makes it impossible for Him to pay for sins. Demonic doctrine, then, seeks to make Jesus Christ a worthless Saviour.

They promote destruction. Destruction of the bodies

and souls of men is another major area of demonic activity. Physical problems which demons can inflict include dumbness (Mt 9:33), blindness (Mt 12:22), crookedness of limbs, paralysis, and torturous diseases (Mk 3:10; Ac 8:7; Lk 13:11, 16). Mental derangement is also within their power (Mk 5:4-5; Lk 9:37-42). The moral impurities of the Canaanites seem to have been traceable to demon activity (Lev 18:6-30; see also Deu 18:9-14), and we know that Satan can tempt believers to immorality (1 Co 7:5).

The war against the souls of men was illustrated by our Lord in His teaching about the worthlessness of self-reformation (Mt 12:43-45). The believer is in a constant spiritual warfare, his enemies being Satan and his demons (Eph 6:12). Notice that this verse teaches the organization and ranking of demons and "their world-wide way over the present . . . spiritual and moral darkness."[4]

In the tribulation period, the destructive power of demons apparently will reach a climax. The judgment called "the first woe" seems to be inflicted by demon-insects (Rev 9:1-12). Their origin is from the "pit of the abyss" (vv. 1-2, ASV), which, according to Luke 8:31, is the abode of the demons. The description of the locusts that ascend out of the smoke from the abyss is certainly not one of ordinary locusts. Indeed, they should be described as demons who take the form of these unique locusts (see also Rev 9:11).

The work of these demon-locust creatures is to torment the bodies of men living at that time, with a bite like that of a scorpion. The agony will be so great that men will attempt to destroy their bodies completely through suicide, but God will not permit this (v. 6).

The judgment that follows involves an army of horsemen

numbering two hundred million (Rev 9:13-21). This may be an army of human beings, or it may be made up of demons. At least the weapons of destroying one-third of the remaining population of the earth are the elements of hell: fire, smoke, and brimstone (v. 17). Whatever be the agency of judgment, the result is a continued unrepentant attitude on the part of those who escape. Their activities include demon worship, idol worship, murders, sorceries, fornication, and thefts (vv. 20-21). The word *sorceries* means magic potions and drugs. Thus demon worship results in demon ethics which destroy life itself (murders), the bodies of men (drugs), marriage (fornication), and the sanctity of property (thefts). People and society will become the special targets of the destructive activities of demons in these coming days.

They promote delusion. Satan's thrust with respect to the world is that of deception (Rev 12:9), and his emissaries, the demons, carry out that purpose. This activity seems to be related most specifically to deceiving the governments of the world. The curtain is drawn back on this in Daniel 10:13, 20. Leupold says:

> Bad angels, called demons in the New Testament, are without a doubt, referred to here. In the course of time, these demonic powers gained a very strong influence over certain nations and the government of these nations. They became the controlling power. They used whatever resources they could muster to hamper God's work and to thwart His purposes. . . . We get a rare glimpse behind the scene of world history. These are spiritual forces at work that are far in excess of what men who disregard revelation would suppose. They struggle behind the struggles that are written on the pages of history.[5]

In the tribulation days, demons will be active in this respect again (Rev 16:13-14, 16). They will be employed by Satan, the beast (Antichrist), and the false prophet to spread deception to the kings of the world so that the nations will gather together at Armageddon. Leaders of these nations will probably think they are doing the correct thing, though actually they will be acting under the strong deception of demonic activity.

This particular activity of demons seems to span all of history. Thus we would have to conclude that they are working in this way today among the nations of the world. (One must be careful not to attribute demonic influence only to "enemy" nations or opposite political parties!)

THE CHRISTIAN'S DEFENSE AGAINST DEMONS

As with many subjects, the subject of demon activity is viewed by many Christians from extreme viewpoints. A few regard the matter as insignificant, acting as if demons did not really exist. More today are oversensitive to demons, seeking a demon under every stone and attributing everything evil that happens directly to demons. They often view themselves as special targets of demonic activity, though in reality they are only flattering themselves into thinking this might be so. Or they sometimes think that they are particularly discerning with respect to possible demon-working in the lives of others. Again they flatter themselves into thinking of themselves as special spiritual giants. Demon activity is very real and will increase as we approach the end of the age, so what are the normal defenses which a believer may use every day?

First, it is important to remember that almost anything Satan can do may be duplicated by other means. Evil in our own lives may be satanically induced, but it is likely more often initiated by our own sin nature. Even psychic phenomena may have explanations other than attributing them to demons. This is not to diminish the importance of knowing what Satan can do, but it is to attempt to make us realize that there are usually several causes in any given action, none or any of which may be satanic.

Second, a believer should never dabble in or flirt with the occult. God warned His ancient people against this (Deu 18:10-11), and the New Testament example of the experience of the believers at Ephesus is most instructive. Some had continued for as long as two years to practice magical arts and consult books of magic. Finally, when they were shocked into burning these books because of a startling confrontation with the demons by Paul, then "mightily grew the word of God and prevailed" (Ac 19: 20). This is certainly one area where it is exceedingly important for the Christian to be "simple [unmixed] concerning evil" (Ro 16:19). Those who have been delivered from demon possession or oppression are the first to insist that they have nothing to do with such practices or anything associated with them from then on.

Third, "let not the sun go down upon your wrath: neither give place to the devil" (Eph 4:26-27). While there is a righteous anger, Paul in these words forbids the believer to prolong it beyond sunset lest he brood over it and stimulate and exaggerate it into personal anger and sin. This admonition is followed by the more general statement not to give place to the devil. The two are connected, for excess of wrath will give opportunity to the enemy to gain an advantage. This is probably one of the most important defenses against satanic activity that the believer can use, and it is one that must be used daily to be effective.

Fourth, do lean on the power of the indwelling Christ and Holy Spirit. Satan or demons cannot gain ultimate victory over believers, for their destinies are guaranteed by God who cannot lie. However, the question is frequently asked as to whether or not a Christian can be demon possessed. Usually the answer given has been negative because of the indwelling of the Holy Spirit in the life of a believer. The argument is that the Spirit and a demon cannot both possess a person; therefore, since a Christian is indwelt by the Spirit, he cannot be possessed by a demon. Today, however, many are saying that believers can be possessed by demons, and some are regularly practicing casting out demons from Christians. What do the Scriptures say about these questions?

The phrase "to be possessed with demons" does not occur outside the gospels. However, this does not necessarily prove that there was no demon possession except during the earthly ministry of Christ. Passages usually cited to show demon possession of believers are: 1 Samuel 16:13-14; Luke 13:11-16; Acts 5:3; 1 Corinthians 5:5; 2 Corinthians 11:4 and 12:7. Upon examining these passages, one has to admit that they do not conclusively prove that believers can be demon possessed, if they prove it at all. Actually none of these verses actually say that a demon or demons possessed a Christian. An evil spirit tormented Saul, but the base of operation (whether from outside or inside Saul) is not stated. Luke apparently attributes the woman's deformity to a demon ("a spirit of infirmity"), and the Lord calls her "a daughter of Abraham" (Lk 13:16). However, it is debatable whether this means that she was a believer or merely a member of the chosen people. In any case she was not a Christian in the post-Pentecost sense of the word. It was Satan, not demons, who filled Ananias' heart (Ac 5:3). Nevertheless, this is probably the strongest proof that a believer may be controlled by demons from within, for this is the same expression as is used of the filling of the Spirit (Eph 5:18). The discipline of 1 Corinthians 5:5 involved delivering the believer over to Satan, which leaves unspecified Satan's base of operation (see also 1 Ti 1:20). The "different spirit" of 2 Corinthians 11:4 (ASV) is not a demon any more than "another Jesus" in the verse is a demon. It is "another gospel" which brings a spirit of bondage (Ro 8:15). And finally, 2 Corinthians 12:7, though referring to a demon who afflicted Paul, does not specify that the base of operation was from within Paul as if the demon possessed or indwelt him.

Surveying the evidence, one is forced to conclude that there is no clear statement of demon possession of a believer after Pentecost. Yet 1 Corinthians 5:5 seems to allow for it, since presumably if Satan can fill a believer's heart (Ac 5:3), he could send a demon to do the same. It is also not without significance that there are no commands in Acts or the epistles to cast out demons from believers.

How can we put these facts together? Here are two suggestions. First, we should discard the phrases "demon possession" and "demon indwelling" when speaking of these possibilities in relation to Christians, for we tend to read into those terms the same ideas that we put in "Spirit indwelling" (i.e., a permanent residence within the individual). Neither Satan nor demons can ultimately have victory over a believer, though apparently they may dominate or control a believer's life for a time. A believer may be delivered to Satan "for the destruction of the flesh," but the spirit will "be saved in the day of the Lord Jesus" (1 Co 5:5). Whatever relationship Satan or demons may have to a believer during this life, it cannot be permanent or eternal.

Second, the indefiniteness of the New Testament concerning the base of operation of demons in relation to believers and the lack of specific commands to exorcise demons from believers may provide a clue to successful war on demons. Demon activity should not be treated by exorcism but just like any other sinful opposition. In other words, the believer should treat demon molestation like temptation or the activities of his own sin nature. Pinpoint the source of attack; examine himself to see if there is any rebellion against the law or will of God; confess any and all known sin; and rely on the power of the indwelling Spirit. Demon activity can be fought successfully by these means and without theatrics, whether the demon operates from within or from without the believer. Even if exorcism seems called for in some unusual instance, the exorcist cannot prevent demons from attacking the same person again, for no human being can guarantee to completely bind demons or send them into the abyss where they would be confined permanently. Paul says we wrestle, or struggle, against the powers of darkness, and that is a lifelong conflict (Eph 6:12). Therefore, the believer must be alert (1 Pe 5:8); be clothed in the armor of God (Eph 6:13-18; and maintain vigorous physical, mental, and spiritual health (Ro 12:2; 2 Co 10:5; Phil 4:8).[6]

One final word: for the unbeliever who is possessed or afflicted by demons, there is only one means of deliverance and that is faith in Christ as Saviour (Mk 5:18-19; Ac 16:18-19).

10

The Question of Evolution

FOR MANY, to believe in creation as taught in the Bible is to believe in ignorance or, at least, in something completely outmoded. But I do believe in the biblical account of creation and with good reason. The alternative, evolution, not only has failed to prove its claims but at best can present only a very weak case. Theistic evolution, the intermediate position, also fails to satisfy. Creationism offers, even today, a reasonable and accurate account of the origin of man and the world.

SOME ALTERNATIVES

In the attempt to reconcile the teachings of evolution with those of the Bible, four alternatives have been suggested to ease the tension and resolve the difficulties that exist between them.

First, there are those who accept the apparent contradictions between evolution and the Bible as real and attempt to believe both viewpoints. Although this would seem to be a logical impossibility, it is essentially the position of theistic evolution which holds that God created all things

This chapter, with minor changes, is reprinted with permission from Charles C. Ryrie, "The Bible and Evolution," *Bibliotheca Sacra* 124 (January-March 1967): 66-78.

through the processes of evolution. Actually, this view-point is not acceptable either to the Bible-believing Christian or to the evolutionist. The Bible states clearly that man was created out of the dust of the ground (Gen 2:7). This could not refer to or include a former animal ancestry, since it is to dust that man returns—and this is not a return to animal state (Gen 3:19). Furthermore, the first man of the Bible was made in the image of God and thus bears no resemblance to evolution's first men.

Evolutionists, too, are dissatisfied with the idea of the-istic evolution, since to admit supernaturalism at any point is to directly counter their theory. Charles Darwin him-self wrote: "I would give absolutely nothing for the theory of natural selection if it requires miraculous additions at any one stage of descent."[1] More recently, Julian Huxley affirms that supernaturalism "runs counter to the whole of our scientific knowledge. . . . To postulate a divine inter-ference with these exchanges of matter and energy at a particular moment in the earth's history is both unneces-sary and illogical."[2]

Second, there is a very popular solution today which ac-cepts evolution but allegorizes the Bible. This approach seemingly allows one to accept the conclusions of evolution and still retain the thrust of the Bible. The allegorizing always involves the first eleven chapters of Genesis, but soon it also includes other parts of the Bible, especially the miraculous. The general ideas of Genesis 1-11 are accepted, but the factual details are rejected. Admittedly, there are many Bible scholars who follow this line of thinking; not-withstanding, it is unacceptable for several important rea-sons.

First, it is purely subjective. Who is to decide what

portions are not to be understood plainly and thus to be allegorized? Why stop with Genesis 1-11?

Second, it is dishonoring to God. If evolution is true, then the "allegory" which God allegedly gave in those early chapters of Genesis is an entirely inaccurate one, and one can only conclude that in giving it God was either untrue or unintelligent.

Third, this concept is in direct conflict with the teaching of many other parts of the Bible. Aspects of creation are mentioned in Luke 3:38; Romans 5:14; 1 Corinthians 11:9; 15:22, 45; 2 Corinthians 11:3; 1 Timothy 2:13-14; and Jude 14. Allegorizing Genesis will of necessity affect the interpretation of these other passages.

Fourth, it discredits the authority of Jesus Christ, for He accepted the account of the creation of Adam and Eve (Mt 19:4; Mk 10:6) and the historicity of the flood (Mt 24:38; Lk 17:27). If His words cannot be trusted in these particulars, how can anyone be sure they can be trusted in other matters?

A third basic alternative is to accept evolution and reject the Bible. Many actually do this, though few are willing to state it quite so blatantly.

A fourth possibility is to accept the Bible fully and plainly with the necessary consequence of rejecting evolution.

Some Data from Evolution

The word *evolution* means change, development, movement, or process. It has a completely legitimate use, as in the sentence, "There has been considerable evolution in the field of communications." But when used in connection with the theory of evolution, the word means more than development. It also includes the idea of origin by

natural processes, both the origin of the first living substance and the origin of new species. That there has been
development in many areas of creation no one denies
(micro-evolution), but that this development has also included the production of new species of more complex and
intricate form from less complicated substances (macro-
evolution) is open to serious question. Ordinary development should not be confused with the origin of species.

Mutations and natural selection. This is the basic and
most important proof that evolutionists advance for their
theory. Mutations are sudden variations which cause the
offspring to differ from their parents in well-marked characteristics. Natural selection causes the survival of these
new forms and accounts for general biological improvement. Concerning this process, Huxley writes that "not
only is it an effective agency of evolution, but it is the
only effective agency of evolution."[3] William S. Beck of
Harvard Medical School stated, "Random mutation produces the variations that Darwin was talking about and
mutation is, as far as we know, the only source of genetic
variability and hence of evolution."[4] John T. Bonner also
affirms that mutation "is really the factor of fundamental
importance. Since mutation means a chemical change in
the gene structure, all progressive advancements must ultimately be by mutation, and all that can be done by recom-
bination is to shuffle what is given by mutation. Gene mutation provides the raw material for evolution, and recom-
bination sets this material out in different ways so that selection may be furthered by being provided with a whole
series of possible arrangements."[5] So basic is this proof that
one may safely conclude that if it can be questioned, evolution itself can be.

There are some important questions that must be asked about the proof from natural selection and mutations.

First, does not the fact that this proof is based on a circular argument weaken it considerably? Notice Huxley's admission: "On the basis of our present knowledge, natural selection is bound to produce genetic adaptations; and genetic adaptations are thus presumptive evidence for the efficacy of natural selection."[6] In other words, natural selection produces mutations, and mutations guarantee natural selection, *but neither can be proved by itself.*

Second, are not mutations harmful? Theodosius Dobzhansky, an authority in the field of genetics, admits that "most mutants which arise in any organism are more or less disadvantageous to their possessors. The classical mutants obtained in Drosophilia usually show deterioration, breakdown, and disappearance of some organs." He also acknowledges that "the deleterious character of most mutations seems to be a very serious difficulty."[7] Since beneficial mutations are not able to be observed, scientists can only speculate or hope that somewhere and somehow during the supposed long process of man's evolution the necessary beneficial mutations did occur. Given enough time, they say, anything could have happened, including helpful mutations. Whether this is so or not we shall test later.

Third, where do new genes come from? Mutations are alternate forms of existing conditions, but new forms have to be produced if evolution is to occur. Protozoa, for instance, do not have teeth. Where, then, did the genes come from which produced our teeth if we evolved from protozoa? Does the evolutionist have an answer to this basic problem? Hear Laurence H. Snyder, a famous geneticist: "As to the origin of genes, we know very little, although it is tempting to speculate."[8]   H. Graham Cannon of Manchester University states: "A fact that has been obvious for many years is that Mendelian mutations deal only with changes in existing characters, never with the appearance of a new functioning character. . . . No experiment has produced progeny that show entirely new functioning organs. And yet it is the appearance of new characters in organisms which marks the boundaries of the major steps in the evolutionary scales."[9]

Fourth, does natural selection really guarantee improvement? Of course, it must do so; otherwise, if a substrain survived, it would soon die out and there could be no evolution at all. J. B. S. Haldane answers: "In fact, natural selection with evolutionary consequences has only been observed where men have created drastically new conditions which impose a heavy selection pressure."[10] *Natural* selection is hardly proved when it can only be demonstrated under *imposed* conditions.

Fifth, if neither beneficial mutations, the production of new genes, nor natural selection has ever been observed, then does not this basic evidence for evolution rest on faith rather than observed fact?

It should be noted that not all scientists, not even all evolutionists, accept the argument from mutations and natural selection as being conclusive. Earnest A. Hooton, Harvard's famed anthropologist, said: "Now I am afraid that many anthropologists (including myself) have sinned against genetic science and are leaning upon a broken reed when we depend upon mutations."[11]

After one hundred years of the theory of evolution, a British scientist summarized the present state of knowledge in this revealing way:

If mutation, which is the only form of hereditary change of which we have definite evidence, is always change in genes already present, it would at first sight seem that we have here no basis at all for understanding the evolution of novelties in the organization of the body. For their evolution we surely need new hereditary factors, not change in those already present. But we must remember that conditions in the body and in the hereditary material are extremely complex. Possibly changes in the distribution of enzymes in the body, if they were somehow brought about, might cause new differences in rate of growth of parts. . . . It is hard to see how redistribution of its enzyme could be brought about by mutation of a gene, but, in view of the complexity of the conditions in the body, it may perhaps be possible. Also, it is not impossible that new genes may be evolved. . . .

These suggestions are purely hypothetical. For the present we cannot say more than that novelties of organization undoubtedly occur in evolution; that they are essential to the increase in complexity which is associated with progress in evolution; that we have no accurate knowledge of the details of their evolution.[12]

Fossils. The question of fossil men (rather than fossil animals) is of far greater significance to the Bible believer, since it is the allegation of evolution that man is very old and that he evolved from prior brute forms. In contrast, the biblical account of creation insists that Adam and Eve were the first human beings, that they were sinless, that they subsequently sinned, and that the resultant effect on the entire race has been one of degeneration. According to the biblical account, Adam and Eve could not have been the climax of some evolutionary process which included various kinds of subhuman ancestors. Incidentally, the theistic evolutionist is on the horns of a dilemma with regard to the creation of Adam and Eve. Even if he succeeds in injecting evolution into the biblical record of the creation of Adam, it is impossible to do so with Eve; and if God created Eve, as the Bible declares, as a direct act of creation, why not allow Him to have done the same with Adam?

Again some serious questions must be asked with regard to the fossil evidence.

First, does the fact that the fossil argument is a circular one weaken its force considerably? *The Encyclopaedia Britannica* admits: "It cannot be denied that from a strictly philosophical standpoint geologists are here arguing in a circle. The succession of organisms has been determined by a study of their remains buried in the rocks, and the relative ages of the rocks are determined by the remains that they contain."[13] This is more than a philosophical point, for the actual pragmatic approach of geology is to date the strata by the fossils found in them and to date the fossils by the strata in which they are found. This procedure can scarcely assure precise results.

Second, are other methods of dating really as reliable as they are purported to be? Concerning the radiometric and fluorine methods of dating: "It must be stressed that the above method [radiometric] and also the fluorine method . . . do not afford any *absolute* dating for fossils."[14] Of the uranium-lead methods another scientist writes: "Geologists have been somewhat disappointed in the uranium-lead methods because of the many instances where the results are contradictory, inconsistent, or unreasonable."[15] Carbon 14, which the average layman thinks can measure accurately for any length of time, begins to have an important margin of error after several thousand years. Furthermore, recently at Westinghouse laboratories the rate of decomposition was artificially altered by three percent.

Third, why has the fossil evidence produced no intermediate forms? It would seem reasonable to expect that somewhere among the many fossils that have been found there would have been discovered at least one transitional form. Instead, the earliest fossils of each group exhibit all the features that distinguish the group to which they belong. The importance of this matter to evolution has been stated clearly by Sir Wilfrid Le Gros Clark (Oxford University); "That evolution actually *did* occur can only be scientifically established by the discovery of the fossilized remains of representative samples of those intermediate types which have been postulated on the basis of the indirect evidence."[16] Of the clarity of this indirect evidence, Alfred S. Romer of Harvard University has written: " 'Links' are missing just where we most fervently desire them and it is all too probable that many 'links' will continue to be missing."[17]

Fourth, does not the evidence from fossil men seem a bit scanty for the conclusions that are drawn? Perhaps the most notorious of all fossil men is *Pithecanthropus erectus,* found in Java in 1891-92. It consisted of a part of a skullcap, a fragment of a left thighbone, and three molar teeth. These fragments were found within a range of fifty feet and over a year's time. Concerning this particular find the *Britannica* concludes: "Additional evidence must be presented before a reliable hypothesis can be constructed."[18]

The Neanderthal race is also considered to be essentially human (though probably degenerate). At any rate, these remains do not prove any evolutionary sequence in the development of man. "Neanderthal remains provide a substantial reminder that there is not an inexorable sequence in skeletal development leading continuously from primitive to modern."[19] A medical doctor told me once that Neanderthal men could easily have been ordinary men who had been afflicted with rickets.

Fossil men do not provide evidence of transitional forms leading to *Homo sapiens.* Indeed, today all fossil men are being classified by most into the single genus—*Homo.*

The necessity of faith. Scorn and ridicule are often heaped on the Christian for having faith, and the image is projected that this is opposed to true science. Seldom is creationism presented as a plausible explanation; rather it is portrayed as an emotional, unscientific, blind faith. Occasionally one finds scientists who state the matter fairly. For example, Harry J. Fuller and Oswald Tippo of the University of Illinois write in their text: "Some people assume, entirely as a matter of faith, a Divine Creation of living substance. The only alternative seems to be the assumption that at some time in the dim past, the chance association of the requisite chemicals in the presence of favorable temperature, moisture, etc., produced living protoplasm. . . . Actually, biologists are still as far away as they ever were in their attempts to explain how the first protoplasm originated. The evidence of those who would explain life's origin on the basis of the accidental combination of suitable chemical elements is no more tangible than that of those people who place their faith in Divine Creation as the explanation of the development of life. Obviously, the latter have as much justification for their belief as do the former."[20] In other words, the evolutionist does not know how life originated, so that whatever he accepts about the subject, he does on the basis of faith.

Faith is also required to accept other parts of the theory of evolution. Concerning one explanation as to the origin of the dawn horse, George Gaylord Simpson says: "In the nature of things this hypothesis cannot be ruled out categorically and some respectable scientists support it. Nevertheless it is so improbable as to be unacceptable unless we can find no hypothesis more likely to explain the facts."[21] Huxley recognizes that the odds against producing a horse by chance are tremendous, and yet he concludes, strictly by faith: "No one would bet on anything so improbable happening; and yet it *has* happened. It has happened, thanks to the workings of natural selection and the properties of living substance which make natural selection inevitable."[22] Concerning the development of the vertebrates from the invertebrates, the famous Hooton declares in a most unscientific manner: "All this is complicated, obscure, and dubious. Anyway there evolved from the invertebrates a tribe of animals which, by hook or by crook, acquired backbones."[23]

Other data. Other alleged evidences for evolution are often cited more frequently in the popular presentations of evolution rather than in technical journals and textbooks. They are: (1) embryonic recapitulation (the human embryo passes through the various stages of evolution in the womb), (2) serological tests (blood precipitates show the relationship of species), and (3) inheritability of acquired characteristics.

Concerning the first, C. H. Waddington (University of Edinburgh) says: "The type of analogical thinking which leads to theories that development is based on the recapitulation of ancestral stages or the like no longer seems at all convincing or even very interesting to biologists."[24]

The results of the blood tests, conducted by George Nuttall of Cambridge in 1904, are so inconclusive that they may be regarded as proving nothing. Indeed, they proved that hyenas are more closely related to cats than cats are to themselves, and pigs are closer to cats than dogs are.

Generally speaking, the inheritability of acquired characteristics, known as Lamarckism, though accepted by Darwin and used by him whenever natural selection failed him, is not considered a good explanation for evolution by most biologists. It appears in popular presentations of evolution such as those one sees with regularity in *The Reader's Digest,* but it has against it the obvious difficulty of suggesting a conceivable means by which, for instance, a man's biceps can become so developed as to modify the genes of the body and transmit the larger muscle to his children.

The necessity of time. When evolutionists are faced with these basic lacks in the evidence for their theory, they retreat into the explanation that all of this happened over long periods of time and, although we cannot observe these transmutations today, anything could have happened given enough time. Huxley, for instance, explains: "All living things are equally old—they can all trace their ancestry back some two thousand million years. With that length of time available, little adjustments can easily be made to add up to miraculous adaptations; and the slight shifts of gene frequency between one generation and the next can be multiplied to produce radical improvements and totally new kinds of creatures."[25] The average person will readily accept a statement like this because he suspects that two billion years is a long enough period of time to cover anything happening by chance.

This idea is one that can be put to the test mathematically. Could natural processes, operating according to the laws of chance (and without supernaturalism there is no other alternative), be expected to produce that which evolution requires in two or more billion years? Bolton Davidheiser, whose doctorate in biology is from Johns Hopkins, has worked out a most damaging analogy in regard to this matter of chance operating over long periods of time which shows clearly the incredibility of the evolutionist's claims. The basic mathematical formula is found in William Feller, *An Introduction to Probability Theory and Its Implications*.[26] He bases it on the well-known statement commonly attributed to Thomas Huxley to the effect that if a million monkeys were permitted to strike the keys of a million typewriters for a million years, one might by chance make a copy of a Shakespearean play. He then sets up the experiment with certain controls in order to be able to treat the facts mathematically. For example, the monkeys are given typewriters with only capital letters, seven puncuation marks, and a spacing key. They type twenty-four hours a day at the speed of twelve and a half keys per second. Instead of a Shakespearean play, the experiment requires them to type only the first verse of Genesis (in English!). How long would it be expected to take the monkeys to do this according to the laws of chance operating within these few controls? Dr. Davidheiser answers as follows:

"The length of time [it would take is indeed] . . . quite beyond our comprehension, but an illustration may help. Think of a large mountain which is solid rock. Once a year a bird comes and rubs its beak on the mountain, wearing away an amount equivalent to the finest grain of sand (about .0025 inch in diameter). At this rate of erosion the mountain would disappear very slowly, but when completely gone the monkeys would still be just warming up.

"Think of a rock not the size of a mountain but a rock larger than the whole earth. Try to think of a rock so large that if the earth were at its center its surface would touch the nearest star. This star is so far away that light from it takes more than four years to get here, travelling 186,000 miles every second. If a bird came once every million years and removed an amount equivalent to the finest grain of sand, four such rocks would be worn away before the champion super simians would be expected to type Genesis 1:1.

"Of course this is quite fantastic, but it is evident that a million monkeys would never type a Shakespearean play in a million years."[27] Similarly, to believe the idea that lifeless matter could evolve by chance into the life we know on earth in a billion years or in a couple of billion years is also fantastic.

In summary, it seems clear that evolution lacks the mutations, new genes, kind of selection, fossilized transitional forms, and time required to support its theory.

DATA FROM THE BIBLE

While it is not the purpose of this discussion to investigate all the possibilities in the interpretation of the creation account of Genesis, some of its salient features are worth noting.

The God of creation. At least seventeen times in the first chapter of Genesis God is mentioned as Creator. Although it should be obvious, it is still necessary to point out that this is not some impersonal force but the same God whom the writer of this portion knew. In other words, the Creator is said to be Moses' God, whom Moses already knew as a personal, living, miracle-working God. Even if one holds to the documentary hypothesis, the God of this section must be understood as the same God who was known to the supposed writer or editor of these chapters, and this too excludes the idea of His being an impersonal something. Moses would have had no trouble believing in special creation, knowing from experience what he did about God.

The process of creation. It is popular today to say that the important truth in Genesis is who created, not how He created. But even a cursory look at the section will reveal quickly how glib such a statement is. God "created," "made," "said," "called," "set," "formed," "caused," "took," "planted," and "blessed." His creative activity is described by these verbs. Furthermore, the section gives the order of creation "day" by "day." Too, it records God's work of creation from start (1:1) to finish (2:1). In other words, the Genesis account tells us the how, the order, and the completeness of the process of creation.

The time of creation. There are certain relevant facts in relation to this question of the time of creation. First, Ussher's (1581-1656) scheme of dating written over three centuries ago is obviously not a part of the inspired text of Scripture.

Second, the demarcation of time sequences in terms of "days" does not begin until 1:3. This means that verses 1 and 2 may cover an indeterminably long period of time. Whether one considers verse 1 the account of an original creation, or a topic sentence for the chapter, or whatever, does not affect this point. It seems, too, that the translation of the first verb in verse 2 does not materially affect the point either. If one translates it "became" and understands some sort of catastrophe between verses 1 and 2, there is obviously an undetermined length of time in the two verses. If one translates the verb "was," this would simply be stating a condition of the earth at that time, whether a changed condition from verse 1 or not, and this could still include a long period of time within both verses. Either of these interpretations may or may not be connected with the casting out of Satan from heaven.

Third, seven days are marked off in the account, all of them by a number, and all but the seventh by the additional phrase "evening and morning." However long one considers these days to be, it is important to notice that man was created on the sixth day and is therefore of recent origin in comparison to the other aspects of creation, including the animals.

Fourth, the results of the flood and their effect on the world as we see it today must be a part of anyone's total picture of creation.

Fifth, an act of creation would most likely include the appearance of age in the object created. Diamonds made in the laboratory appear to be as old as diamonds found in the earth, but in reality they are of recent origin. The wine that Christ created at Cana (John 2) looked as if it had gone through the long process involved in making wine, when in reality it was only minutes old when it began to be used. The account of the creation of Adam and Eve indicates mature people who only appeared to have passed through the normal time-consuming processes of growth. How much of this God did in other areas of His creation we do not know, but that He did it in several instances is clear.[28]

These are some of the most relevant facts revealed in the Bible concerning creation. Since the truthfulness of the account is attested to in other parts of the Bible and by Christ Himself, since the Bible itself has been shown to be true in other areas (particularly in the matter of fulfilled prophecy), and since the data of the theory of evolution is built on circular arguments, is full of gaps, and requires something in the nature of blind faith to believe, the choice of what to accept about creation really should not be too difficult to make.

Notes

Chapter 1

1. Tacitus *Annals* 15.44.
2. For provocative reading on this subject see Jacques Ellul, *Violence* (London: SCM, 1970).

Chapter 2

1. John W. Sloat, "Let's Abolish Capital Punishment," *Pulpit Digest* 50 (January 1970): 46.
2. "After Capital Punishment, What? *United Evangelical Action* 24 (May 1965): 17.
3. For these and similar statements, see Gerald H. Gottlieb, "Capital Punishment," *Crime and Delinquency* 15 (January 1970): 2-11.
4. Hugo A. Bedau, ed., *The Death Penalty in America* (Garden City, N.Y.: Doubleday, 1964), esp. chap. 6.
5. "Report of the Committee on Resolutions," *Yearbook of the American Baptist Convention, 1958* (American Baptist Convention, 1958).
6. Jacob J. Vellenga, "Is Capital Punishment Wrong?," *Christianity Today* 4 (October 12, 1959): 7.
7. J. Duncan M. Derrett, *Law in the New Testament* (London: Darton, Longman, & Todd, 1970), p. 183.
8. Charles S. Milligan, "A Protestant's View of the Death Penalty," in *The Death Penalty in America,* ed. Bedau, p. 178.
9. Dwight Ericsson, "The New Testament Christianity and the Morality of Capital Punishment," *Journal of the American Scientific Affiliation* 14 (September 1962): 77-79. See also the weak interpretative paraphrase in *The Living Bible* at Ro 13:4, "The policeman is sent by God to help you."
10. William G. T. Shedd, *A Critical and Doctrinal Commentary upon the Epistle of St. Paul to the Romans* (New York: Scribner, 1879), p. 378.
11. F. L. Godet, *Commentary on St. Paul's Epistle to the Romans* (Edinburgh: T. & T. Clark, 1883), 2:311.
12. J. Edgar Hoover, "Statements in Favor of the Death Penalty," in *The Death Penalty in America,* ed. Bedau, p. 134.
13. Felix Kessler, "The Gun," *The Wall Street Journal* 179 (June 6, 1972): 1.

CHAPTER 3

1. Demosthenes *Theomneustus and Apollodorus Against Neaera* 122.
2. William Fairweather, *The Background of the Epistles* (New York: Scribner, 1935), p. 30.
3. Solomon Schechter, *Studies in Judaism* (London: Adam & Charles Black, 1896), 1:389.
4. Albrecht Oepke, " γυνή (Woman)," in *Theological Dictionary of the New Testament,* ed. Gerhard Kittel and G. Friedrich (Grand Rapids: Eerdmans, 1964), 1:784.
5. Archibald Robertson and Alfred Plummer, eds., "First Epistle of St. Paul to the Corinthians," in *The International Critical Commentary* (Edinburgh: T. & T. Clark, 1911), pp. 324-25.

CHAPTER 4

1. Herman L. Strack and Paul Billerback, *Kommentar zum Neuen Testament* (Munchen: Oskar Beck, 1922), 1:312-20.
2. John Murray, *Divorce* (Philadelphia: Orth. Presby. Church, 1953), pp. 47-48.
3. John Murray, "Divorce," in *Baker's Dictionary of Theology* (Grand Rapids: Baker, 1960), p. 169.
4. John Duncan M. Derrett, *Law in the New Testament,* p. 379.
5. Alfred Edersheim, *The Life and Times of Jesus the Messiah* (Grand Rapids: Eerdmans, 1943), 2:354.
6. George Salmon, *The Human Element in the Gospels* (London: John Murray, 1908), pp. 130-31.
7. Sylvester Joseph Hunter, *Outline of Dogmatic Theology* (London: Longmans, Green, 1900), 3:416.
8. W. K. Lowther Clarke, *New Testament Problems* (New York: Macmillan, 1929), pp. 59-60.
9. James Hope Moulton and George Milligan, *The Vocabulary of the Greek New Testament* (Grand Rapids: Eerdmans, 1949), pp. 695-96.
10. Alan G. Nute, "The Pastoral Letters," in *A New Testament Commentary,* ed. G. C. D. Howley (Grand Rapids: Zondervan, 1969), p. 510.

CHAPTER 5

1. A. N. Triton, *Whose World?* (London: Inter-Varsity, 1970), pp. 182-83.

CHAPTER 6

1. Joseph Fletcher, *Moral Responsibility: Situation Ethics at Work* (Philadelphia: Westminster, 1967), p. 34.
2. Harvey Cox, ed., *The Situation Ethics Debate* (Philadelphia: Westminster, 1968), p. 11.
3. Editorial, *The Rocky Mount (North Carolina) Telegram* (January 13, 1967).

4. Cox, p. 10.
5. Joseph Fletcher, *Situation Ethics: The New Morality* (Philadelphia: Westminster, 1966).
6. John A. T. Robinson, *Honest to God* (Philadelphia: Westminster, 1963), p. 105.
7. Ibid., p. 32.
8. Joseph Fletcher, *Situation Ethics,* p. 26.
9. Ibid., p. 105.
10. James A. Pike, "*Agape* Is Not Enough," in *The Situation Ethics Debate,* ed. Harvey Cox, p. 199.

Chapter 7

1. Carl F. Keil and Franz Delitzsch, *The Pentateuch* (Edinburgh: T. & T. Clark, 1880), 2:124.

Chapter 8

1. Carl F. Keil and Franz Delitzsch, *Biblical Commentary on the Old Testament* (Edinburgh: T. & T. Clark, 1878), 2:134-35.
2. Bruce K. Waltke, "Old Testament Tests Bearing on the Issues," in *Birth Control and the Christian,* ed. Walter O. Spitzer and Carlyle L. Saylor (Wheaton: Tyndale, 1969), pp. 10-11.
3. Joseph Addison Alexander, *The Psalms* (Edinburgh: Thin, 1873), p. 231.
4. Mildred Krentel, *Melissa Comes Home* (Chicago: Moody, 1972).
5. Cited by E. H. Gifford, *The Epistle of St. Paul to the Romans* (London: John Murray, 1886), p. 159.
6. Klaas Runia, "Abortion Issues," *Eternity* 22 (February 1971): 21.
7. Spitzer and Saylor, eds., *Birth Control and the Christian,* p. xxvi.
8. Carl F. H. Henry, "Abortion," *Christian Heritage* 32 (February 1971): 25.

Chapter 9

1. Charles J. Ellicott, *The Pastoral Epistles of Paul* (London: Longmans, Green, 1864), p. 54.
2. Victor H. Ernest, *I Talked with Spirits* (Wheaton: Tyndale, 1970), p. 38.
3. Brooke F. Westcott, *The Epistles of John* (London: Macmillan, 1892), p. 75.
4. Charles J. Ellicott, *St. Paul's Epistle to the Ephesians* (London: Longmans, Green, 1868), p. 147.
5. Herbert Carl Leupold, *Exposition of Daniel* (Columbus, Ohio: Wartburg, 1949), pp. 457-58.
6. See Ernest.

CHAPTER 10

1. Robert E. D. Clark, *Darwin: Before and After* (London: Paternoster, 1950), p. 86.
2. Julian Huxley, *Evolution in Action* (New York: New Amer. Lib., 1964), p. 20.
3. Ibid., p. 35.
4. William S. Beck, "The Riddle of Life," *Saturday Evening Post* 230 (May 10, 1958): 92.
5. John T. Bonner, *The Ideas of Biology* (New York: Harper, 1962), p. 64.
6. Huxley, p. 43.
7. Theodosius Dobzhansky, *Evolution, Genetics and Man* (New York: Wiley, 1955), p. 150.
8. Laurence H. Snyder, *Principles of Heredity* (Boston: Heath, 1951), p. 332.
9. H. Graham Cannon, *The Evolution of Living Things* (Manchester: Manchester U. Press, 1958), p. 92.
10. J. B. S. Haldane, "The Theory of Natural Selection Today," *Nature* 183 (March 14, 1959), pp. 710-13.
11. Earnest A. Hooton, *Apes, Men and Morons* (London: George Allen & Unwin, 1937), p. 118.
12. G. S. Carter, *A Hundred Years of Evolution* (New York: Macmillan, 1958), pp. 184-85.
13. *The Encyclopaedia Britannica*, 1956 ed., 10:168.
14. Alan H. Brodrick, *Man and His Ancestry* (New York: Fawcett, 1964), p. 122.
15. William L. Stokes, *Essentials of Earth History* (New York: Prentice-Hall, 1960), p. 22.
16. Wilfrid Le Gros Clark, *Discovery* (January 1955), p. 7.
17. Alfred S. Romer, *Genetics, Palaeontology and Evolution* (Princeton: Princeton U., 1949), p. 114.
18. *The Encyclopaedia Britannica*, 1957 ed., 2:52.
19. Ibid.
20. Harry J. Fuller and Oswald Tippo, *College Botany* (New York: Holt, Rinehart & Winston, 1961), p. 25.
21. George Gaylord Simpson, "The Great Animal Invasion," *Natural History* 49 (April 1942): 206.
22. Huxley, p. 42.
23. Earnest A. Hooton, *Up From the Ape* (New York: Macmillan, 1936), p. 56.
24. C. H. Waddington, *Principles of Embryology* (London: George Allen & Unwin, 1956), p. 10.
25. Huxley, p. 41.
26. William Feller, *An Introduction to Probability Theory and Its Implications* (New York: Wiley, 1950), 1:226.
27. Bolton Davidheiser, *Evolution and the Christian Faith* (Grand Rapids: Baker, 1969), p. 363.
28. See the excellent discussion of this point in John C. Whitcomb, *The Early Earth* (Grand Rapids: Baker, 1972), pp. 29-33.